Purposely

PROTECTED

Kept in All Thy Ways

SHYTAZHIA HAMILTON

FORWARD BY SANDRA COLEMAN

Excerpts from New King James Version Study Bible by Max Lucado.
Printed in the United States of America.
For more information, or to book an event, contact: Oracles Den
den4oracles@gmail.com
http://www.oraclesden.com
ISBN - Paperback: 9798371658487
First Edition: January 2023

CONTENTS

Acknowledgments

I want to express my deep gratitude and appreciation to my family for all your patience and understanding while completing this assignment. My husband Ace, thank you for all your sacrifices, support, and pushing me to keep going when I needed it. My children, Joevarn, Azavion, and Zyrei, for bearing with me and stepping in to help me when I need you. My mother Joanie B, for being my go-to person and jumping in whenever you see a need. I want to thank my grandmother, Janie Mae, for being the example of a God-fearing woman and intercessor in my life. Thank you, grandma, for sharing your stories and collaborating with me on this project. Thank you for your late-night prayers and for covering over for this entire family. Every tear you dropped and every sweat that has fallen to your brow is not in vain. My spiritual sister Sandra Coleman, thank you for prayers, covering, mentoring, and seeing me as God sees me. I thank God for putting us in the path of one another.

-I love you all

Forward

Some friendships you will encounter may only sometimes be pleasant and have come to an end. There are those whose company is more profound than just a cordial how are you; it's when the soul has connected you. That's my friendship or my sistership with ShyTazhia. Coming into this life, this young lady and I have gravitated toward one another. With that, I've learned from her over the years as she poured out her heart to me. She didn't come with a cute story but one that was a bloody walk and produced such a mighty warrior and survivor. I had watched the literal hand of God evolve her into the masterpiece He created when He spoke her name from her mother's womb. Tay (as I call her) has a story that we all can, and I'm sure, will benefit from. You will see in this book someone who came from brokenness to becoming whole, from victim to victorious. This book will change your life! I am super proud of you, Tay, and continue to share your story with us. The world is waiting on YOU!

-Prophetess Sandra Coleman

Preface

I have always had a passion for books. Ever since I was a child, I always found myself with a book in my hand. I was the most introverted child in the house because I often stayed in my room writing, reading, and sometimes drawing. Sometimes, my brother and I would write songs and poems just because that's what we liked doing. We would write music, record it on the old cassette player, and play it back like we knew what we were doing. He would do the verses, and I would sing the chorus. Sometimes we would play around with the music and have some friends join us. I was good in other areas and became interested in them as I got older. Still, I never realized that the one area that was my place of peace as a child would be my place of purpose as an adult.

As I got older and started experiencing all that life had to offer, I forgot about writing and focused on survival. In December 2017, I started getting tired of working for other people, being on their time, and making them wealthy while I just made ends meet. It became so intense I thought about it all the time that I hated clocking in for work. In January 2018, I resigned from working with the department of corrections, my husband and I relocated, and we started a trucking corporation. It gave me more time at home to spend with my children, make money without being stressed, and nurture the unborn child we had on the way. However, even though finances began to flow better than before, that was more of my husband's thing. I was there to help and support him with everything. I still felt incomplete, but not quite the same as being at work because I wasn't affected by the different stresses. In addition, I had my baby in October 2018, and I can see that the Lord gave me time to readjust to life with our newborn baby.

In January 2019, the Holy Spirit started inspiring me to write again. I have gone through so much that I knew I had plenty to share with the world. One night after I put my children to bed, I stayed up cleaning and talking to the Lord because that was my quiet time with Him. I was talking about how I felt and began to ask about the push that I was feeling to go back to writing. Different book title ideas started flowing when I took a moment to just sit in silence. I wrote down the titles I received, then saw images of children's books and asked, "Children's books too?" I smiled and said, "Okay, Lord, but I don't know how to start." I didn't get any more

downloads that night, but three days later, I got the clarity I
needed on a Sunday morning.

After the worship service, the Apostle introduced a
prophetess to the congregation that was bringing forth the word
that morning. Once the prophetess concluded her message, she
began to minister to people individually according to what the
Spirit of God was saying; in other words, she was flowing in the
prophetic. She made her way to me and just paused and looked
at me as I held my hands up to the Lord as an act of surrender.
The prophetess began to tell me, "you need rest, you are not a
procrastinator, but you need rest." "There are books inside of
you." Then she proceeds to say, "and yes, children's books too."
I couldn't do anything but drop my head down and laugh. "You
have a story to tell, and the world needs to hear it," she
continued. "Don't worry about making it perfect, but for now,
just start writing, that's all." "If you don't have a mentor or
someone that can help you with any questions or anything,
come get my information after church," That was the end of the
message the Lord sent to me.

Once I began to put the vision in motion, I had difficulty
focusing because of life. The trucking business was a good
source of income. Still, as an independent company that has

yet to establish any business credit, almost everything was being taken care of with out-of-pocket expenses. So instead of keeping the promises of God in mind, I started focusing on the thought that we need another income stream. I went from starting a blog and adding merchandise to my website to having a clothing drop shipping company. I was walking in total disobedience. I was flowing with my ideas but had to learn that every thought and vision was not for that moment. Some things are for later, and some are by condition, meaning that some things only come to pass when you align yourself accordingly.

One morning, I was praying about the stresses from the boutique while I was on the way there to open up, and I heard the Spirit of the Lord say, "WRITE ."I started hearing the song, Handwriting on the wall by Dottie Peoples. I was singing the song without realizing it, and then I caught myself. I stopped in shock because it was a moment, just like when someone has to think about what they are thinking. Then I wondered how that song relates to me. The only thing I could think about was the warning God was sending to King Belshazzar from the unbodied handwriting of the message on the wall.

Furthermore, I heard the word "WRITE" in my spirit repeatedly. This time, it was coming to me with force; the more I heard it, the more forceful it became. The best way to describe how I heard it was like someone knocking on an old heavy wooden door with the iron-designed knocker hitting louder and louder. It didn't take much for me to give in because the fear of God gripped me, and my response was a shout, "Okay, okay, Lord, I will write ."Then suddenly, it stopped.

I never heard Him say anything about the store, although I saw it. He sent prophets my way that said the same thing at different times about my boutique, but it was not for that season. As much as I wanted to keep my store open, I closed it down because things weren't moving the way I was praying for them due to my moving out of order. That's what visionaries do sometimes when we don't understand the order of how God wants things done. It's not a complete NO, but we must learn the seasons and when to move into the visions He has shown us. I did not follow the specific instructions sent from heaven, which was a hard lesson I had to learn.

After going through all of that, I realized I wasn't in control of anything the way I thought I was. Although it may appear as wasted time and money, it taught me to trust, have faith, and move according to God's word. So now, I submit myself to the instructions given to me for my life as a published author. I present myself to you as a living testimony, in the utmost transparency, with no filter, raw and with the truth. I pray that this book reaches who it is supposed to and impacts the hearts connected; in Jesus' name, Amen!

Introduction: Grandma's Testimony

Ever since I was a little girl, I knew there was something different about me, and God chose me. I always stood out from those that were around me. The Lord has been with me as far back as I can remember. Still, knowing what I know now, I understand that God gives angels charge over us, and I just knew that the Lord assigned an Angel to me that always talked to me and protected me. I didn't realize what was going on with me initially because I was just eight years old when it started. Still, as I was getting older, the Lord made himself known to me, and I understood He was a good father, friend, provider, and protector.

When I was eight, the Lord started allowing me to see spiritually. He started speaking and giving me messages to tell others. The Lord would commission me to do certain things, and there was always someone there to bless our household by sending money, food, or items for me to return to momma. For instance, if the Lord gave me a message to give someone, and once I did it, they would provide me with something and tell me to take it back home as thank you. Momma used to tell me to stop asking people for stuff, but I would just explain that I only did what the Lord told me to do, and people would give me things. I could tell who appreciated my obedience to the Father and didn't. Some people used to look at me in disregard because I was young, but I knew they knew what I was saying.

Everywhere that I went, I lifted the precious name of Jesus. Sometimes I would just sing and give God glory because I love Him, and He was my friend. Some people didn't mind, and some were annoyed by my presence. I believe the spirits that people carried were annoyed and uncomfortable by the presence of God with me. When I became a young adult, some people said things to me and about me openly. Some pretended to like me but didn't understand that my God didn't leave me ignorant. I saw the spirits that operated in them; if I didn't see, the Lord would let me know what was going on with them.

As I continued to grow into a mature woman physically and spiritually, the Lord would show me things before they happened. He would even let me hear conversations of people talking about me. He needed me to be mature enough to not react to my emotions and to keep certain things to myself that He revealed to me. I moved from the south to the north when I got old enough to work. I started my own family, and with everything I had going on with life, the Lord remained faithful and unchanging toward me. One day, as I was walking home from work, the Holy Spirit told me, "do not eat the food on the stove." I asked the Holy Spirit why and again, he said, "do not eat the food that's on the stove; something is in it." When I went to the house, it smelled like food was cooking on the stove. I walked in to see where everyone was and when I saw my husband, Franklin, I asked him, "did he mix up the food on the stove?" He replied, "no, you know I don't touch the pots when you put food on; that must've been Missy stirring in the pots." When Franklin responded, it confirmed what the Lord had already revealed to me: Missy and Franklin were having an affair. Missy was Mary's daughter, whom I knew as an associate who pretended to be my friend when I knew she always felt some type of towards me. The Holy Spirit instructed me to take the pot and throw it out because Missy was trying to poison me.

I didn't say anything to Missy because the Lord hadn't released me, so I followed His lead and kept my mouth closed. Another time I came home from work, the Holy Spirit said, "go look underneath your bed." When I did, there was a jar that appeared to be some type of barbecue sauce with ground black pepper. The Lord told me, "take it and throw it into the sewer drain." He wanted me to throw it into the sewer drain underneath the curve, but I took it to Pastor Oneal to see what he would say. Once I got it to Pastor, he told me someone wanted me dead. So many attempts did not work, and those same people were beginning to think that I was a witch but little did they know, nothing can take over me when God is on my side. The Pastor told me not to open it because it might blow up in my face. Still, I already opened it, nothing happened. Leaving the Pastor, I walked while praying and tossed it into the sewer drain.

One day the Lord gave me an open vision of an attack and allowed me to see myself. In my mind, I thought the Lord was letting me know that someone was going to kill me. I kept asking the Lord why this would happen to me, but He never answered my question. He just told me to call my aunt and ask her to help me wash and clean my house. With the mind frame that I was about to be taken away, I sat the children down and talked to them about taking care of one another and sticking together. I told them to listen, do what they were supposed to do, and make sure not to give anyone a hard time. Weeks passed, and everyone on the block celebrated the Fourth of July. Music was playing, food was cooking, some were sitting under the tree drinking, and people were dancing and having a good time. My big boys were playing basketball with Mary's big boys the last time I checked, and I walked into the house. Franklin kept calling for me to come out and get a drink, but I didn't want to drink what the rest of them were drinking, so I just took a sip of what he had and walked back into the house. A few minutes later, Mary knocked on my door, saying the boys were outside fighting over the ball. I told her to just take the ball from them and put it in the house. I guess that was not what she wanted to hear; even with that, I knew she did not like me. I knew she was pretending to be my friend, she felt like I think I am better than the rest, and she knew that her daughter Missy was having an affair with Franklin. Mary was upset that I did not fuss or say too much to the boys and stormed off. Minutes later, there was a knock on the door. Two of my children were in the house, so they came with me when I walked to the door. When I answered the door, I saw it was Mary, and then a can of lye was thrown at me.

Some of the lye got into my eyes, and I ingested some. Mary ran off to hide, and Franklin came to the house, looking for the pistol. I was pointing to my bosom, whispering, "right here, right here," and he took it and ran off. Mary went to hide somewhere, and I don't know who, but somebody found her and called the police. I was taken to the hospital by ambulance and was pronounced dead three times. The last time I died, I could hear my two little girls run to the doctors, yelling and telling them that I was dead. When they came back with the doctor, I was sitting up in bed. I remember the fluid was running out of my mouth, and suddenly, God blew the breath back into me, and I just inhaled and was back. When they returned to the room, I was sitting in bed. Another time that I left, I was riding in a chariot. The chariot passed the trees, going up the hills and the mountains. The horses were just going; it was just the angel sitting in the chariot with me. I had the privilege of seeing the beauty and the splendor of heaven. I did not want to come back, but the Lord said not yet, and I had to return, but the doctors thought that they were calling the shots when they told me they would give me three months to live.

The doctors told me that if I lived, I would be completely blind. However, I was still here and with my vision after two and a half months. My vocal cords were eaten up from lye, so when I spoke, the whole voice wouldn't come out; only a whisper would come out. I asked the doctor if I could go home, and the doctor responded, "how are you going home when you cannot eat or swallow? Your insides are all eaten up," He continues, "you can't walk or eat like normal." I said, "yes, I can, the Lord said that I can," and the doctor said, "here you go with all that God stuff again." "I don't know what kind of God you have that you think you can go home and still live, but we'll see in the next couple of weeks." So after that conversation, the Holy Spirit spoke to me and told me, "when the nurse comes and leaves the vaseline on the counter, I want you to get it and eat it." I said surprisingly, "eat it?" He repeated again, "eat it." A few minutes later, the nurse walked in with the vaseline, and I asked her if she could hand it to me. The nurse said, "I can't give it to you because you can't take all kinds of medications." I told her, "I can have it; the Lord told me to tell you to give it to me." The nurse, in return, said, "I'll tell you what, I'll sit the vaseline down on the counter, and you can do what you want with it, but do not call my name." She put it down and went her way, and I grabbed the vaseline and ate the whole jar. When the nurse returned, she asked, "did you take it?" and I said, "yes." I don't know if she ever said anything to the doctors, but after eating the vaseline, I could produce more of a sound, a more potent whisper. Later that night, the Lord told me, "a missionary will come to your room with blessed oil in her hands, tell her I said to give you the oil."

When she came to the hospital, the visiting hours were over, but she told them she needed to come up. When she came up, she made the wrong turn and came to my room. The missionary had a bottle of holy oil in her hands about the size of my pinky finger, and I told her the Holy Spirit said to give the oil to me.

She said, "oh no, the oil is for someone else." I told her, "the Lord said it's for me." The woman said, "I can bring you some more tomorrow because I already promised someone this bottle, I just made the wrong stop, and I have to go up to the next floor." I said, "Okay then, that bottle is supposed to be for me but okay." She left and had to come right back. She said, "Well, I guess I had to come back because the elevator would not let me off." The woman handed the bottle to me and left. The Holy Spirit told me, "grease yourself down, grease your mouth and drink the oil." I did everything that the Holy Spirit told me to do, everything. They said I wouldn't live, but I could get up and walk out of that hospital one day. I was allowed to leave for a few days, but the doctors kept telling me I wouldn't return if I left. However, when I was gone, I took care of myself by the grace of God, and I made it back to the hospital, to my same room. The doctors couldn't understand me and said they had never seen a person like me. Seven doctors were standing over me and looking at each other puzzled because I was surviving without food and drinking water. I was simply obedient to God and the instructions He had for my life. Fortunately, one day they decided to let me go home permanently because there was nothing else they could do. I exceeded the time they gave me, and the Lord cared for me. After some time, one of the ladies from the church said to me, "Sis Hamilton, the Lord said you can eat whatever you want, "whatever you want to eat, we are going to eat together." I went from vaseline and oil to a soft diet to solid foods.

The Lord gave me total healing. The skin grew back as it once was, my voice was back, and my organs healed. Today I am eighty-four years old, and nobody can tell me anything different other than that with Christ, all things are possible. His love, grace, and mercy kept me when the enemy thought he had me. The same mantle and grace that the Lord has placed on me, He has given double to my granddaughter Tazhia. Divine grace and protection shall be her portion as she fulfills God's will for her life, in the mighty name of Jesus!

CHAPTER 1

Mantle To Mantle

God communicates with us in various ways. Because we are always moving about and are distracted so easily when we are awake, he gets to us best by giving us dreams. When we sleep, our bodies are resting, but our spirit man is alert. When we sleep, our spirit is open to His spirit. The Lord gives us warnings, deliverance, and even ideas through dreams. Sometimes He may just want to show us something to spark our curiosity so that we may seek Him. He will also use this form of communication with His prophets, and truth be told, this is a way that some begin to come into the knowledge of who they really are. Prophets tend to have dreams or night visions that eventually come to pass. Some dreams are symbolic, and some dreams are literal.

In my case, this is what has been happening to me. At a young age, God started giving me dreams or night visions. I had no clue what was going on with me, but the more He gave me dreams over the years, the more intense they became. This was just one of several ways God revealed the woman He created me to be.

I started having night visions at eleven, dreams that literally felt like reality. My first-night vision was of a tornado that split into five separate tornadoes. I wasn't a part of what was happening, but I watched everything. I've never seen a tornado other than on television, but to see one that was just as good as seeing one up close and personal and to see it split into five. At that age, that was so weird to me.

Furthermore, about a month later, my family and I were in the den watching television, and the news came on. A tornado that touched down in another state split into five, just as I saw it in my dream. Instantly, I was compelled to the screen in amazement. Excitedly, I started telling my family that this was what I dreamt about, but no one paid attention, so I just got quiet. The older I got, the more my night visions became more intense. Not only the night visions but day visions. I started to see things happen before they actually happened.

A few years later, at about fifteen, I walked to a friend's house around the corner from where I lived because this was where the friends in the neighborhood would typically hang out.

Just minutes after being there, I started having an uneasy feeling that wouldn't let up. I ignored the feelings that I was having because I thought that it was just me and didn't know this was the Spirit of the Lord communicating with me. The more I ignored it, the stronger it became. So, I went into the room with the girls to watch television, and some others went next door where the boys were. That unsettling feeling was at its strongest because now God had decided to let me hear a conversation that was not in the same room as I was. I said nothing to no one, and no one said anything to me, yet there was a conversation going on, and someone was lying on me. By this time, I just decided to go ahead and leave, so I made my way out the front door and down the steps, but as soon as I hit the road, I heard someone yelling my name, "T-A-Z-H-I-A, "T-A-Z-H-I-A." I turned around, thinking, who was yelling my name like that? It was Nya, one of the girls who walked to the house next door where the fellas were at. I started walking towards her as she was walking towards me, and the first thing Nya said to her mouth was, "were you sitting in the house talking about me?" I somewhat laughed, thinking this must've been what I was feeling. I replied to her, "I didn't say anything about anybody." Next comes the accuser, Bianca trying to talk over me like she was right "so you didn't say that she was probably over at the next house in your boyfriend's face?" By this time, everyone in the other houses heard all the commotion and started coming outside. I looked at one of the girls and asked her, "did I say anything about anyone in the house?" She replied, "no, you weren't really saying anything." I looked back at Nya and said, "I told you, that girl is lying; why would I even say that about you?" At this point, Nya was about to jump down Bianca's throat. Hence, Bianca decided to walk towards me like she was about to prove a point in front of everyone. Unfortunately for her, as soon as she started all that loud talking and pointing in my face, I blacked out on the girl and punched her as hard as I could. All I could see was her. Everything else got dark and blurry. This was the third time Bianca stirred up a situation and put my name in it, so I took everything out on her, the old and new. In the middle of our fighting, I felt somebody pulling on me, saying, "move, Tay, let me finish her." Bianca was on the ground trying to fight back, and I was on top of her, and it was hard to snap out of it, but eventually, I moved out of the way anyways. I was so angry at myself for two reasons: I should've left, and I allowed this girl to pull me out of character.

I didn't try to stick around because I was so mad, so the best thing was to go home like I started to. On the way home, I was walking and thinking about how weird I felt because of everything that had happened. I felt confused and crazy simultaneously, and I was thinking, how in the world did I know something was about to happen? I thought back to God, but again I had no idea that things like this could happen to a person.

As a young adult, I never heard anyone speak of spirituality and experiences like this other than my grandmother. She shared her personal spiritual experiences with my siblings as we were growing up. It really didn't get much of my attention when I was younger because the understanding wasn't there. Still, the older I got, the more I started to experience, and the more my compacity began to expand. Additionally, I started enjoying and valuing my grandmother's stories because I realized she was grooming and imparting them to me. She was imparting wisdom, knowledge, and understanding to me.

I don't recall any church members speaking on encounters or visitations from heaven other than my grandmother. Truth be told, the people always looked at my grandmother funny or rolled their eyes at her whenever she spoke of her genuine relationship with God. She didn't care, though, because she knew what was and wasn't afraid to say what needed to be said.

The woman I am becoming now, I can see that I am much like my grandmother. My grandmother has day and night visions; she always talks about how the voice of God speaks to her, how the Holy Spirit forewarns her, gives her insight, and comforts her. From the young age of eleven to fifteen, God started to interrupt me with His Spirit. I had no clue what it was, but all I knew was that life was getting weird and unexplainable.

CHAPTER 2

Outer Darkness

God knows what He's doing when He gives His chosen people life-changing experiences. The Father is intentional about the experiences He allows us to have because it's for a greater purpose. Many people had near-death experiences and made it out because of God's will for our lives. Some had the privilege of experiencing the location of hell and heaven; however, my experience showed me just who Christ is.

One night, as I decided to lie down, God allowed me to have a personal experience in the spiritual realm. I don't know why but I decided to lie on the front room sofa instead of getting in my bed. However, after I fell asleep, I noticed I was in a dark place. It was dark without any lighting, and I was just there. Suddenly, I saw a black silhouette, a demonic spirit in the form of a man standing in front of me. This form had no features about it. I couldn't see any details other than it was blacker than the black around us. I was terrified, and there was nowhere I could go or nothing I could do now. Within a split second, the dark spirit went from just standing in front of me to being face to face with me, and I mean close enough that I felt the heat from it.

I began to feel extremely hot; I couldn't scream, fight, or anything. I couldn't move and couldn't even begin to explain why. I was just there, stuck in one position, and could not do anything but observe everything that I could. I thought that I had died and gone to hell. Next, the demon began to speak to me and was trying to convince me to give up with its lies. It told me, "you mind as well give up; you already belong to me; there's no need to fight ." It kept repeating itself to me, and the more it spoke, the weaker I noticed I was getting. Deep shallow breaths were all I could take because now I was hypo-ventilating and literally felt like life was leaving me. A part of me accepted that this may be it for me because I was weak at this point. However, in my weakness, I was made strong.

"And He said unto me, my grace is sufficient for thee: for my strength is made perfect in weakness. Most gladly therefore will I rather glory in my infirmities, that the

power of Christ may rest upon me". 2 Corinthians 12:9 KJV.

Suddenly, I heard a voice that was unquestionably distinctive from any other I'd ever heard. Although I didn't see anyone else, I knew it was the voice of Christ himself without a doubt in my mind. He came in without an introduction of who He was or an explanation. Immediately, I felt a sudden peace come over me. His voice was calm, peaceful and hopeful but with authority. Just when I thought I would be in eternal damnation for the rest of eternity, I heard the voice of Christ say, "go back to the verse you learned in Sunday school." As soon as I listened to the instruction, that gave me strength and hope. So, I started repeating the scripture.

Jesus said to him, "Away from me, Satan! For it is written: Worship the Lord your God and serve him only." Matthew 4:10 NKJV

As I kept repeating this scripture, I noticed that the demon was losing its grip on me. Then I heard the voice of Christ with another instruction; he said, "say the name, Jesus." I repeated the name Jesus like I meant business because I was determined not to lay there and die. "Je-sus, Je-sus, Je-sus," I said, and oh, was he angry now. Just like an enemy that wants to get to you so bad, but because it was something or someone blocking them from getting to you, all they could do was get angry and holler out.

Similarly, the enemy was mad because he thought he would have me. It growled in my face with so much intensity but couldn't do a thing to me, and then he disappeared. My spirit was returned to my body, and I was soaking wet in sweat when I woke up. My clothes and my pillow were wet, and my body was fatigued. I couldn't just sit right up; I took my time to sit up, and once I did, I couldn't do anything but just sit there for a min thinking to myself, what in the heck just happened to me.

I managed to get up but staggered as I walked to the phone to call my pastor. My co-pastor answered the phone, and I explained what had just happened. What was the coincidence that he would say he already knew? "One of the deacons called and said that someone was fighting a demonic spirit, but we didn't know who it was until you called." "You don't even know; we've been praying for you." I couldn't do anything but cry because I did not understand what happened and was still in shock. I was shaking and did not want to go back to sleep the rest of the night. At the time, I was unclear where my spirit was taken to, but now I feel sure I was in the outer darkness. There was nothing around but absolute darkness!

But the son of the kingdom will be cast out into outer darkness; there will be weeping and gnashing of teeth. Matthew 8:12 NKJV

Then the king said the servants, bind him hand and foot, and take him away, and cast into outer darkness; there will be weeping and gnashing of teeth. Matthew 22:13 NKJV

And cast the unprofitable servant into outer darkness: there shall be weeping and gnashing of teeth. Matthew 25:30

I was so happy and grateful that the Lord came through and saved me just when I thought that was it for me. I can see now that He was beginning to train and prepare me by teaching me warfare with the word of God. It is our weapon, our sword, and will work against Satan and his dominion. He also showed me to trust in the power of the name of Christ Jesus.

And take the helmet of salvation, and the sword of the Spirit, which is the word of God. Ephesians 6:17 NKJV

Many people try to rationalize if Jesus is the son of God, messenger, or prophet. I can only speak on what I know for myself, and there is absolutely nothing no one can say or do to change my mind from believing in the power of the name Jesus. Some people say the name of Jesus because of what others have told them, and then some know without a shadow of a doubt what type of power the name Jesus brings. The moment I began to say in the name of Jesus, the demon lost its control over me. The fact that he got angry about it and left was all I needed to witness to know the truth for myself.

Jesus answered and said to him, "Blessed are you, Simon Bar-Jonah, for flesh and blood has not revealed this to you, but My Father who is in heaven. Matthew 16:17

We must get to the point of knowing the Lord for ourselves and not just going off of what other people taught us. When you are ready for Him to reveal the truth, you have to ask Him, and He will reveal it. All it takes is an open heart and sincerity because He wants to show people the truth, but He will not intrude against your will. If you want it, He will give it. If you are thirsty for it, He will quench your thirst. All I can say is remember what you ask for!

CHAPTER 3

False Potential

When I was younger, I made many mistakes due to a lack of knowledge. There were some things I needed to be taught regarding life and relationships, and I had to learn them on my own as I went through them. Experience will teach a person something better than anybody ever can. Experience will give a person wisdom, and wisdom will provide them with patience. When people understand the importance of patience until God sends the right person, they will enjoy their singleness and not settle for anything coming their way.

As women, we take on projects thinking that we can turn someone into what we hope they will become because we see potential in what is being displayed falsely. When we first meet someone, they sweep us off our feet with an illusion of who they really are. An abuser will never show their true colors all at once, so when you start to see the red flags, it's best to pull away because it worsens with time. There are levels of abuse! I was in a relationship that I should have let go of. I saw the red flags, yet the potential and possibilities had me dealing with someone insecure and delusional. Arguments turned into pushes that eventually turned into punches.

Often God will allow the opposition to come up to present opportunities to draw one closer to Him. In this case, the resistance I was facing was with the relationship I was in. Everything was good with us until I became pregnant with my firstborn, and I guess in his mind, he probably was thinking, got her now! The first red flag that I noticed was signs of jealousy. There were always insecure questions and comments portrayed as joking, but I knew deep down it wasn't a joke. I stayed in this relationship because I kept looking at the potential and the possibility that things would improve. Not realizing that me staying with him only made things worse. I did not have the wisdom to know that the only way to make someone respect me was by first respecting and loving myself. Because of potential and possibilities, I accepted the type of behavior given to me. I didn't say anything to anyone about the things that started happening, mainly because nobody knew. He created most of his shenanigans when we were alone. My family was close-knit, so he never tried anything around them. Secondly, I was

pregnant, and I thought it was embarrassing to mention
something to someone, especially to my family. I was young,
just finished high school, and I didn't want my ending to be like
the average female my age. What I was holding on to was
precisely the potential and the possibilities.

CHAPTER 4

Pregnancy Battles

When I discovered I was pregnant, I was going on three months and had the worst morning sickness up until four and a half months. At the time, the father of my unborn child was so supportive, loving, and understanding. He was there for every doctor and emergency room visit and went through the motions with me. Again, I just knew that my ending would be utterly different from those in my age bracket. As time passed, I began to see a change in the man I thought would be the one. I was too young and didn't have the wisdom to understand that there are levels when one is in a relationship with an abuser. The thought of being in love with a happy ending blinded me from the flags waving in my face.

Shortly after entering my second trimester, I noticed a change in his character. He was becoming jealous, and it seemed as if I had to walk on eggshells because it was getting to the point that I didn't know if I should say certain things around him. After all, I didn't know what exactly he would have a problem with next. Next, I couldn't go anywhere without him going. At first, I thought it was cute because, in my mind, I thought he was really into me and our situation. Still, after a while, it was becoming uncomfortable. For instance, he didn't have anything to say if I was with certain people like my mother, grandmother, or aunts.

After the morning sickness stage subsided, I wanted to go out with my cousins for a break from the house. Two of us were pregnant just a few weeks apart, and we wanted to go out to eat and go to the movies. Nothing major, just a typical night out for a pregnant girl. For some reason, that was a problem that I needed help understanding. I was pregnant, my bump was beginning to show, and I was lazy to the point that I didn't want to do much but eat and sleep; plus, my looks were changing, so I was confused about the problem. However, I wasn't letting this man change my mind because I wanted to get out of the house and get something to eat. The girls were waiting on me in the car. He was following me everywhere, trying to get under my skin so I would change my mind about going and staying in the house with him.

Still, I kept it moving, and he kept going about nothing. When I made it inside the car and shut the door, he opened the door back. So now we are going back and forth with opening and closing the door. My cousin decided to pull off the next time I shut the door. As my cousin started to pull off, he jumped on the car's hood, holding on to the hood. I was highly embarrassed and told him that he needed to go home. I was angry, and even though I kept myself distant for a few days, I eventually forgave him. Again, in my mind, I did not want to be on my own raising a child, and I figured that he would finally change and not even realizing this was the start of something that I did not want.

My Second Trimester

In the middle of my second trimester, my patience started getting thin as the jealousy and accusations grew from what it started out as. It went from delusional comments such as "oh, you were trying to mess with my brother or you going to see your other man?" My mind was nowhere near any of the things he accused me of. I was becoming more focused on my finances, getting things together for the arrival of my baby, and my well-being. I was tired of hearing all the delusions and trying to defend myself from someone who started looking like they had a problem with me. One night, he asked my mother if I could use the car to drop him off at home, and as we were riding in the car, the silence was thick. After a few minutes of pure stillness, another accusation came out of his mouth. "You must have somebody else because you sure are acting funny," he said. I kept silent as I accelerated the gas to hurry up and drop him off. He continued saying whatever the devil was putting in his mind. I was praying within myself because I felt things were about to worsen.

He became angry that I wasn't entertaining him and mushed me in my head. I kept my mouth closed, still praying, and then abruptly, he threw the car into park. Because we were on the same street where he lived, I just got out and ran as fast as I could toward his house so that his mother could hear us outside. Unfortunately, I couldn't run the way I used to because of the belly plus the extra weight. I wasn't close enough to the house before he caught up, pushed me into the dirt, and grabbed me by my head. I don't know exactly what he was saying; I just knew I couldn't put my baby in a situation that could cause me to miscarry. Eventually, he let my head go, and he went into the house, and I walked back to the car, dusting myself off. Thankfully, I wasn't in any pain nor had any spotting. When I got back home, I just showered and went to bed. I didn't mention anything to not one person, but I started weaning myself away from him. Phone calls got rejected, I was doing what I needed to on my own, and I wasn't pressed about him at all.

Three weeks later, I was riding with his sister in town, who also became a close friend of mine. She had to make a stop at her mother's house. As she entered the house, I stayed in the car, but her mother wanted me to come inside so she could see me and the belly. I hesitated at first, but I thought, let me just go in for a quick moment. As I talked to my unborn child's grandmother, trouble walked out of the room. "What are you doing here? I told his mother I was going to get back in the car because I was over all the foolishness. His mother said, "you don't have to leave, and his sister said, "you better not put your hands on her in front of me." When I started walking and making my way out, he grabbed me, and the next thing, I was on the floor right in front of the door. It happened so fast I don't know how I got down there, and then he was pulling me by my right leg and dragging me outside the house. His sister went crazy, and the two started fighting. I couldn't help because I didn't want to get hit in the stomach, but she gave him a run for his money.

Somehow the fight ended up back in the house, and I felt terrible because, I couldn't separate them or even help. Their mother told us to go ahead and leave so he could calm himself down. While we were leaving, he came back outside with his sister's television and slammed it down. He tried to provoke and excite another fight, but we left anyways.

The Last Trimester

I spent most of my last trimester by myself. I wasn't worried or focused on my unborn child's father because the most important thing to me was about ready to make an entrance into my life shortly. As time drew closer, I discovered that He was involved with another female. The way it came out, I could only see God telling me to let this relationship go again. Not halfway, but all the way and wholeheartedly.

One day, a female named Nikki called my mother's house, asking to speak to one of my brothers. "He's not available; may I ask who is calling?' She said, "my name is Ivy," and then proceeded to ask, "you're pregnant by Quan, right?". So now I realize something is kind of off because she's trying to get personal. "What is it to you?" I asked. She says, "I asked because your baby's father and I have been seeing each other for a while." "Oh really?" "You and my baby's father have been seeing each other?" was my reaction. Nikki continued to tell it all, "yes, we have been seeing each other since you were three months pregnant." I kept quiet while she told me everything about me and my relationship. "Yeah, I been talking to him. Whenever I called the house, I would just ask for your brother, and he takes the phone into the room for him." "Mmm, okay," I replied. I remained composed through everything she was saying, and I asked her, "are you finished?" "Nikki said, "I just thought you should know."In my calmest yet most serious voice, I told her, "I got something for you when I catch up with you." Nikki kept going on and on, and I said one last time, "I got something for you when I catch up with you," and I hung up the phone. It wasn't long before I caught them together.

About a week and a half later, my baby's aunt Nita drove me to the store so that I could get something to eat. Before I knew it, I saw Quan coming out of the store with Nikki, and they were getting into her car. She was driving, and he got in on the passenger side. As soon as I saw them, I tried to stay calm, but anger overcame me. Especially after the abuse I went through and the accusations put on me. I told Nita to drive me back to the house. When she did, I couldn't think of anything else but getting back at her like I told her I would, all because she knew everything about me and still went along with it. So, I told my mother I was leaving to do something, and I told my cousin Unique to come. I knew I couldn't do much, so I told my cousin to handle her. At this point, I'm being me and not thinking anything about God and my experiences thus far. I was angry and hurt and allowed my emotions to get the best of me.

Furthermore, we drove to where I knew they would be, and when we pulled up, my cousin got out of the car and started damaging her vehicle. That wasn't what I wanted, so I went back on the promise I made to Nita and Unique, and I jumped out of the car and went to handle my own business and fought the girl myself. I wasn't worried if anything would happen to my baby because I knew everything would be fine, but I blacked out because of how much hurt and anger I had built up. If I had known what I know now, my actions would have been much different, but do I regret it? No, I do not. It was what it was, and I learned from it.

Two Weeks Later

Two weeks passed with Quan and I not speaking or having any contact with one another. In that second week, my mother and I went out to shop, and I started having continuous pains in my lower abdomen. I didn't know better than to think I was in active labor. We drove back to the house so that I could freshen up and get my things. The pain was so excruciating I had to hold on to the wall and stop walking at times. After I arrived and checked into the hospital, Quan appeared shortly afterward. The nurses sent me straight upstairs to the labor and delivery floor, and they told me to change into the gown provided. When they checked my cervix, I was five centimeters dilated. They started the IV with Pitocin because my contractions started slowing down. They set up the stirrups and all the other equipment for delivery, but things began to turn for the worst.

I couldn't feel my contractions anymore, and the Pitocin didn't seem to be helping. The nurses were running in and out of the room, and I didn't understand why. Next, my grandmother walked into the room and came straight to me, saying, "do not let them cut you" When she told me that I was trying to push harder than before, nothing was happening. I was not feeling any contractions to help the baby come down. Speedily, the doctor came in and said, "we have to take you to the operating room." I still was trying to push because I didn't want to have a cesarean. However, the nurses came in to wheel my bed to the operating room. Still, no one explained what was happening with my baby, and I started feeling fearful.

Nita returned to the room; however, I didn't want anyone but my grandmother because I began to feel like I might die having this baby. I asked one of the nurses, "has my water bag ruptured already?" And she looked back at me and said, "you didn't have a water bag." I was even more confused because my water bag (amniotic fluid) had never ruptured. Nita said softly, "Tay, you have dry labor." No one said anything about it or what it even meant. Afterward, I learned that dry labor is when the amniotic fluid is at a dangerously low percentage that can be life-threatening to the baby. Therefore, everything was slowing down because I had no fluids to help the process. They wheeled the bed into the operating room and gave me the epidural. As they laid me down to continue the procedure, I felt a tightness in my chest. The nurses said it was expected, but I could not breathe effectively because of the pressure and tightness in my chest. The nurse put an oxygen tube in my nose as I was panting to breathe, and a few minutes later, I heard my baby's first little cry. As I lay on the operating table, tears just filled my eyes. It was the most precious sound I've ever heard; the sound of life that was created filled my heart with joy. I birthed a beautiful baby boy named Quesaan, who weighed six pounds and twelve ounces. He was healthy, and everything was fine with him.

After leaving recovery, I was placed in another room. The nurses came in to do another part of the post-delivery, which consisted of pushing down on the cervix. This is to help your cervix move past your navel to ensure that the cervix is contracting back to normal size. Unfortunately, this process was turning for the worst for me. As the nurses were pressing down on my abdomen to help it go down, instead of my cervix going down, it started filling up with blood. It was then they realized that I was hemorrhaging. The nurses began to panic because the blood wouldn't stop. They kept moving me from side to side to change the bedding, but every time they changed it, more and more blood came out. The next thing I remember was looking at the ceiling lights, just as in a movie. I was looking up at the lights, and then I would pass out, my eyes would open back up, and I would pass out again. It happened repeatedly. When I opened my eyes again, I saw my friend's mother, Ms. Carolyn, beside the bed, and then I passed out again. I heard a lot of commotion from the doctor and nurses working on me. Over all the noise, I heard Ms. Carolyn saying, "Tay stay with me; you got that beautiful baby waiting on you; stay with me." Fortunately, she worked at the hospital and was on my floor when she saw everyone moving with urgency in and out of the room. She was right there by my side after being told who it was. I heard her words, looked up at her, and passed out again.

I don't remember them getting me stabilized and under control, because I kept going unconscious, and it was just a blackout. All I remember was a couple of hours later, I woke up with an IV in my hand with two different tubes connected, and when I looked up, it was a bag of blood hooked to the IV. "Welcome back, Ms. Hamilton; we almost lost you, girly," said one of my nurses. I was confused and asked her what had happened? The nurse explained that I had lost four pints of blood. I was in Class 3 for hemorrhaging, and Class 4 was the highest. I lost 30 to 40 percent of my total body volume. If it had gone any higher, I would've entered Class 4, which calls for immediate resuscitative help. The strain on my body's circulatory system would've been too great for survival if it would've gone that far but thank God it didn't. I had to get four bags of blood put back into my body.

I couldn't see my baby until the following day because my body underwent a significant shock. They also wanted to ensure the anesthesia was out of my system before I could hold him. However, the very moment I was able to have my son in my arms, I was overjoyed. Every change that I went through was worth it. The first thing I did was see who he resembled the most. I counted his fingers and toes, looked for any birthmarks while checking his body out, and then took his hat off to see how much hair he had. I felt like the heavens had opened over us when I pulled him closer to me to kiss and smell his face. I whispered to him, "Mommy loves you ."Just as I spoke those words, his eyes opened. I am grateful that God kept me here when He didn't have to.

Day four was the day that I was supposed to be discharged, but they had to keep me due to a high temperature. So, because of all my complications, they kept me under observation. My temperature would break, but it eventually went back up. I wasn't breastfeeding, and I didn't know my breast was supposed to stay wrapped up because no one told me I had to; moreover, my breast was gorged. I thought this was why I kept running a fever, but I found out the real reason after being discharged. During my postpartum appointment the next week, I was told that they kept me for a week in the hospital because I had an infection internally at the site of my incision. Anyone else would've used that as a reason to sue the hospital, but I didn't have the strength to go through it. I was just happy to be here with my son.

CHAPTER 5

The Thick Of It

After coming home, I had a hard time healing because my incision was vertical, from under my navel to my bikini area. That type of incision takes a little longer to heal, and also because of the infection that I had within my incision. Quan barely came around for the first two weeks after the baby and I was home even though he was at the hospital from the time I was admitted until the time I was discharged. There were times I would just lay across my bed gazing out of the window and the next thing I would see is his car going right past my house. I really didn't sweat it much because I wasn't trying to have that aggravation in my life like that.

Dealing with the disconnection in my relationship, I was mentally preparing myself to be responsible for another life on my own. On the other hand, Quan started coming around more often about a month after the baby was born. At this point, my baby weight has dropped and I'm starting to get back to myself. When Quan started to come back around on the regular, his thing was that he wanted his family back. Of course I fell for it, I didn't want to be just another black single mother.

Furthermore, about three weeks later, things slowly began to turn again. One morning, my cousin and I went down to social services to get an application to apply for food stamps just to take advantage of the benefits that I qualified for now that I have a child, and came back home to complete it. I looked at it as help to put some extra food in the house, meanwhile, Quan looked at it as if it was some type of revenge on him. He accused me of filing papers for child support and was absolutely wrong. I showed him the application and filled it out while he was there showing him that none of his information was put on the application. I asked him if he can take me to turn it in the next day and he was fine with it. The next morning, we got up and got dressed to take the application back to the social services office. The morning was peaceful; Quan helped me get the baby dressed and helped me carry the carseat as well as the baby bag to the car. The ride was pleasant, we stopped to get something to eat and we talked the rest of the way to social services with no problem. While my baby and I were in the office doing the food stamp interview, he stayed out in the car. I don't know what he was doing, what was going on with him or if he spoke to someone while we were inside, but when we came out he was a different person.

When we came out of the building to get in the car, his composure was just the same as when we were leaving the house. He asked me to drive and I was fine with that. As soon as we pulled out of the parking lot he said in a calm tone "so you went in there to put child support on me?" I looked at him and said, "I just showed you the papers and you are asking me the same thing again". He repeated himself and I refused to repeat myself so I kept quiet. The ride was still and quiet but I could feel it brewing. I was driving and hoping at the same time, that was the end of that. Before I could drive to a place where there were a lot of people, Quan pulled his gun on me and was telling me where to drive. Now I'm praying while I'm driving just in case this day was the day God decides to call my name. He had me drive down this long dirt road that turned into a dead end. I had no idea where I was at, to this day I can't say where this road is at. I got to the dead end and he started with the accusations again. I remained calm while he began to get irate and all I justI prayed and made my peace with God and I just sat and started praying for my baby who was in the back seat sleeping. Whatever demon that had a hold on Quan was trying to get me to act in a way just so it could have a reason to kill me but I remained calm, quiet, and still that I never even shedded a tear. So quiet that the demon inside of him couldn't take it any more and he decided to start slapping me in the face and punching me in the head. Just enough that it wouldn't bruise me and I just sat there and didn't fight back because I knew if this was it for me, I already had my talk with the Lord. He got even angrier and put his gun to my head but instead of pulling the trigger, he hit me in the head with it. At that moment I felt like I blacked out but at the same time I can still hear everything. My head was resting back on the headrest and I couldn't move. After doing all of that, he started to panic. I could hear him saying "Tazhia get up, stop playing get up" while he was shaking me trying to wake me up. The whole while I was out, I was still aware of what was going on. I can't explain it but I knew everything that was still happening. My baby slept through the whole episode of madness. After about ten minutes, I slowly began to lift my head and I can tell he was so relieved. I just sat there in the driver seat with my eyes open looking out the windshield into the woods. I don't remember if I drove back to the house myself or not but I made it back home. When I got back to the house, no one could tell if something just happened or not. I wasn't bleeding, swollen or anything. I walked in the house with my things and he got the baby out of the car. I said nothing to no one. I walked in the house, put my things down in my room, went back to the front and grabbed my baby with his seat and his bag. Quan sat in the den for a while, I guess to see if I was going to say something to anyone in the house. I wiped my baby down, changed him, and took me shower. When I got out he was still in the den sitting and talking to my family like nothing ever happened. I looked him right in his face with disgust and went into my room and shut my door.

It's been weeks since I spoke to him and I was just fine. Everytime he called, I did not feel like talking or being bothered with him. The more I refrained from him the harder he tried. Then he started popping up and his thing was that he wanted to see his son. I would let him see his son but I most definitely was not feeling him. Even if he was at my home, I wouldn't even let my baby be alone with him. This went on for weeks as well and then I guess the enemy decided to be a little more clever. He really had to pull out a good one to even get me to consider. Furthermore, he started trying to take his conversation and cleverness to another level. Quan called one day, crying and saying he was sorry about everything and that he wanted his family. I wasn't moved by his voice or the sniffles that I heard across the phone. A few days went by of the same thing but I still wasn't moved by anything that he was saying and really just didn't want to hear anything else. I ignored his calls for a few days and the next time I spoke to him he said " I went and got us an apartment". My reply was "for what?" He then said, " I told you I wanted my family back and I'm trying to prove it to you". All he got from me was "I don't know about all of that". I pretty much ignored him until I had a huge argument with a family member at the house. That's when I started thinking about giving him another chance after petty arguments kept coming up frustrated at home. I did not give in instantly, I still let him sweat a little more. Then about two weeks later, I told him I'll stay the night with him. It went from me staying the night to staying a few nights and then the baby and I were there for two weeks with him. We were going to church together with his family and his uncle who was the pastor used to counsel us. In my mind, I'm thinking "he's really trying to change".

CHAPTER 6

Manifest

Now, in this day and age and timing, I realize how much the devil himself wanted to kill me. I now know that everything takes place spiritually first before occurring in the natural world. I did not have the spiritual knowledge that I now have. Looking back into everything, detail to detail gives me more insight into what was happening.

Quan and I agreed that we would get up and go to church service Sunday morning, and his sister Nita was coming to pick us up. We got up to get ready for church. I dressed the baby first and was getting his bottle to feed him when Quan went outside to check the mail from the day before. I don't know what happened to him, but he had to be possessed when he walked back in the door. The first thing I noticed when Quan came back was his appearance. He looked like something had taken control of him because his eyes were bugged out of his head and were bloody red. Next, I noticed that he had veins popping out of his forehead and neck as if he was straining. In both corners of his mouth, he had foam and saliva sitting there caked up. I was looking at him like I was facing Satan and thinking, he just went outside for two minutes. Another thing that I noticed was that his voice was different. His voice was a bit deeper, and he spoke more forcefully, as if he had power and authority.

He returned to the house saying, "you've been messing around with my brother and my home boys?" All I could do was respond like it was the dumbest thing I'd heard. I was already praying to God, "Lord, not today; please don't let him start with this mess today." I walked away from Quan with the baby in my arms because I was burping and putting him to sleep. He walked around the house talking to himself like he was having a psychotic episode. When I put the baby down, he came straight to me, looked me right in my eyes, and said again, "you've been messing with my brother and let my homeboys run a train on you?" I don't know where Quan got this information from, but he acted as if he was convinced, or this was made up in his head. I said, "I don't know what you are talking about." Suddenly he just mushed me in my head when I was walking away. I took a deep breath, kept walking, and said, "I am so sick of you putting your hands on me." He kept pushing me, and when I wouldn't respond, he just hauled off and punched me in the back of my head. I just knew that I would have to fight my way out of that house. I felt like it was a situation that he was going to kill me or either I was going to kill him. It was either him or me. That's what I kept thinking to myself because I could feel death in the atmosphere. When he punched me, I turned around and punched him in his face like I was trying to take his head off.

Quan, or should I say the demon looked at me with a smirk and said, "oh, you fighting back today?" He swung again, and I just started going crazy on him, fighting with every bit of strength I had. Physically fighting a demon was pointless because it seemed to be gaining strength every time I swung and did nothing but tire my body out. I didn't know much about fighting in the spirit, so I did what I could. He spoke to me in a weird tone and laughed as if he was all-powerful and mighty, saying, "I'm gonna teach you a lesson." He came at me again and started punching me uncontrollably wherever the punches landed. All I could do was fall and cover my head.

As I said, this demon talked like he was the most powerful thing. I couldn't think at no point of uttering the name of Jesus like the first spiritual experience I had. Moreover, I saw him walk over to the iron and unplug it as he talked. Immediately I screamed out, asking him not to burn me and pleading with him not to burn my face. He kept talking and laughing as he wrapped the cord around his wrist and slowly began to walk my way in the creepiest way ever. I tried to stand but couldn't because somewhere in the fight, my leg got hurt. It wasn't broken, but whatever it was, I couldn't stand on it. When he got to me, he grabbed my hair with one hand and repetitively hit me in the face with the iron. As he was hitting me, I heard him talking to me as a parent would when they chastise their child. Still, I was trying my hardest to cover my face and was not paying attention to what he was saying. He dropped the iron, walked to the closet, and reached to the top. He pulled down a handgun and put the clip into the gun. After being beaten half to death, I didn't even care to live anymore.

Nextly, when he walked over to me, I accepted that I would die in that apartment. He raised his hand and began hitting me with that gun until he was tired. Then he yanked me by my hair to stand up, and I couldn't stand on my leg, so when I dropped, I fell on my baby Quesaan, who was three months old. We just had a blowup mattress on the floor, and when I fell on him, as a typical newborn would, he cried hysterically. When I reached for my baby, Quan grabbed him by the leg, pulled him up off the mattress upside down, and started swinging him back and forth. My son hollered in a way that most people would not even be able to imagine from a newborn. I cried and screamed at Quan and told him to put my baby down. My son's cry was so excruciating that I was ready to give my life in exchange for his.

I took every pain I felt, crawled up on the wall, and stood up. For my baby, that pain was nothing compared to my love for him. When I stood up, I said to Quan, "you can do what you want to me, but you're gonna put my baby down." He looked at me and said, "if you don't make this little bi— shut up, I swear to God I will throw him into the wall." I looked at the wall and limped closer to him to get my baby. Demonically, he laughed, but he put my baby back down. When I got to Quesaan, I picked him up and just held him close to me to comfort him, to let him know that mommy was there. As I began to speak and whisper to my baby, he started calming down, but I wouldn't let him go back to sleep because he was just upside down for about a minute.

I sat with my baby in my arms and didn't want to put him down. The fighting calmed down, and it was time to feed my baby again. I couldn't move like usual, so I had to ask Quan to get his powdered milk and the water jug so I could make him a bottle. After feeding the baby, he went back to sleep, and now that my body was out of that fight-or-flight stage, I had to use the restroom. When I looked over at him, he was sitting there looking at me with a death stare. So I opened my mouth and asked, "can I use the bathroom?" He looked at me like he hated me and said with an attitude, "go ahead." Again, I could not walk, so I crawled to make my way to the bathroom. When I opened the door, the closest thing there was the sink. I pulled up on the sink, held on with some strength, and looked into the mirror. Despairingly, I looked at my face and just broke down and cried. Looking outward, it seemed pretty normal but my eyes were barely open. Both of them! My eyes were so swollen I had a knot on the right side of my forehead, and my nose and lips were big and swollen. My lips looked like Mr. Clump's lips in The Nutty Professor when he was blowing up from the smaller version of him back to the bigger version.

My face was battered. I did not look like the pretty brown-skinned girl I knew. Looking at the girl in the mirror, I saw hurt, despair, and hopelessness. I accepted that I might not leave that house alive, but somewhere inside me, I heard a voice saying "SPEAK." I turned on the water, and with all the hopelessness, strength began to rise. I opened my mouth and said, "God, please get me out of this house; if you get me out of this house today, I promise I will never turn back." I held my cry in as much as possible so that Quan wouldn't hear me. I held on to the sink, trying to keep as much weight off my leg as possible. I lifted my body some to go towards the direction of the toilet, and once I emptied my bladder, I leaned over to the sink to wash my hands. Leaving out of the restroom I had to lean back on the floor and crawl back out of the bathroom.

Once I got back to the mattress on the floor, I sat beside my baby, wondering if God would come through for me. I said nothing to Quan, and he said nothing to me. All of a sudden, there was a knock at the door. It was his sister Nita coming to pick us up for church. As she knocked on the door, Quan walked over to me with the gun in his hand, and he pointed it straight at my head, whispering, "you better not open your mouth." I didn't even try; I sat beside my baby calmly. She knocked for about five minutes and left after not getting any answer. Thank God my baby didn't cry or anything because it was no telling of what would've happened if he did. Nita left without curiosity about why no one was answering the door and knew that we had told her to come and get us that morning. When she left, Quan must've gotten a sense of relief. His attitude changed, and he started acting as if he was concerned about me and how I felt. "Do you need me to get you anything?" he asked as he walked around the apartment. "No," I said. "Are you sure?" "Do you want something to eat?" "No," was my reply again. He went into the kitchen anyway to make me something to eat and came to where I was sitting, put the gun down beside him, and tried to feed me. "Here, eat this," he said. I kept my mouth closed, rejecting the food, not only because I did not want anything to eat but because I knew something was really wrong with this man. It was mind-boggling to me how someone can nearly beat the life out of a person they claimed that they love, attempt to harm their child, and then wants to feed them food. That made absolutely no sense to me. After I kept rejecting the food, his attitude switched back on. Quan started rambling about whatever was coming to his mind, and still, I sat quietly and calmly beside my baby. Next, he started moving around the room like he was searching for something. Eventually, Quan found a notebook, tore a page out, and brought it to me with a pen. He walked back to the chair and sat down with the gun pointed at me, saying, "you are going to write your mother a letter saying you took your life." I sat there thinking this dude can't get any crazier than he already is. With all my bruises and swelling, he thought that somebody would believe I killed myself. I went along with it anyways, but my heart was still calling on Jesus. Quan got up and snatched the paper out of my hand to read it and began to tell me what to change and what to put down on the paper. Like I said, I went along with it anyway without wondering how God would deliver my baby and me out of the hands of Satan.

About an hour and a half later, there was another knock at the door. Once again, Quan looked at me, put his index finger over his lips, and whispered, "you better not say anything," while walking towards the door. This time he was shaken after looking through the peephole. He ran back to the room quietly and grabbed me up by my arm with one hand because he had the gun in the other hand. Forcing me to come into the front room to stand in the middle of the floor. For some reason, my leg wasn't in pain as it was earlier, so I could stand. Quan whispered to me, "that's your cousin Toya at the door." He was in such a panic that it was all over him.

Meanwhile, I'm feeling hopeful now. Quan pulled me by my arm to walk towards the window, and when we got there, he pulled the curtains back and unexpectedly noticed that my cousin's father-in-law, John, was standing there. John yelled out while pointing at the window, "there he goes right there." I remained where I was, and Quan ran from the front room window to the kitchen window. He pulled the kitchen curtains back and saw that my uncle Tee was standing at the window. Tee yelled out, "yeah, he's in there." The whole time, I stood in the same spot, looking at everything without trying to scream or run. I was happy deep down, but at the same time, I kept being prayerful because Quan still had the gun in his hand. Suddenly he had a change of heart and decided to run back into the room and put the gun up. Quan came out of the room, pulled me back in front of the door, and looked back at me. Before opening the door, he had the audacity to say, "be cool," as if my face wasn't battered. I couldn't get calmer than I already was as if that would make a difference when my family saw my face.

Quan opened the door, and I saw my cousin Toya, her husband Monte, Monte's father John, and my uncle Tee all standing at the door. My cousin Toya looked at my face and walked towards me slowly in disbelief. "Oh my God, Tyesha," she said. Toya has always called me by my middle name ever since I can remember. She walked to me because I was still standing there, somewhat traumatized. She gently put her hands up to my face and said, "we came to take you home" "do you want me to take you home to your momma?" All I could do at that moment was utter softly, "please." Toya said, "okay, I'm going to get the baby and your things; you go ahead to the car; grandma is out there waiting." While Toya was talking to me, the guys were already in the house. I just noticed they took Quan into the room, and I heard a lot of commotion. Toya was on her way into the room where the commotion was to get the baby, but she looked back at me to see if I was still standing there. She waved her hand, saying, "go ahead; I got the baby; just go to the car." I turned around to the door and slowly walked out. The pain wasn't in my legs as bad as it was, but my body was hurt. I walked out slowly, reaching to hold onto the wall. My fragile body was barely holding up when I came out of the apartment. I held onto the wall and went down the hall into the blinding sun. I felt like someone who came out of a dark tunnel or an underground bunker. When I got to the car, I noticed other people standing around. I didn't hide and did not feel embarrassed because I wanted the world to see what was done to me. Even one of Quan's uncles was out there. He walked over to where I was and looked at me like he was shocked yet hurt at the same time. He shook his head and said, "Tay, are you okay?" I just said, "yeah, I'm okay now." As he walked off, I heard him say, "Lord have mercy." When I got in the car to my grandmother, she looked at me with so much hurt and anger. "I knew something was wrong, I knew it, I knew it, I knew it," grandma said as she hit the steering wheel. The more my grandmother looked at my face, the angrier she got. While she was speaking, Toya came to hand me Quesaan. The next thing that I saw was Quan coming out of the house. Looking just like he got dragged all through that room he had me hostage in. I thought the most mentally ill thing he could've done, after battering me, asked me if I wanted something to eat and actually try to feed me, but this fool had the nerve to ask my grandmother for a ride. My grandmother paused, looked back at me, and turned back to look at him. She said, "boy, something is really wrong with you," as he stood there looking at her. Then in the most aggravated way, she said to him, "you know what, get in." He got into the car and acted as if he never did anything wrong. I was already convinced that it was something demonically wrong with him. So as we were riding in the car, my grandmother was going off on him. He asked my grandmother to drop him off around the corner from where we lived, and when she drove past that street, he began to panic. I said sarcastically, "what are you nervous for?" He didn't reply; he didn't even turn to look at me. My grandmother went straight to our house, and my brothers and uncles stood outside. He tried to get out like normal, but when my family saw my face, rage overcame them. My brother said to Quan "yo, tell me why my sister's face is like this?" He kept saying, "I didn't do anything to that girl; she did that to herself." I was reaching to get my baby out of the car, and I heard my brother say to Quan "hold on, I'll be right back." I already knew that meant, and so did Quan because fear was all on his face. My brother entered the house and came out with a steel bat, and one of his friends pulled up his shirt to show his gun. Quan took off running, and they took off running right behind him. I wasn't concerned or even cared about what happened to him. I got my child, and I kept moving without a caring bone as I heard everything. When

I got into the house, my mother was livid when she saw my face. She immediately grabbed the phone and called Quan's mother. When his mother answered the phone, my mother said, "So, who do I have to thank for my daughter's face?" They went back and forth for a minute. I heard my mother say in response to something that was said to her, "what the hell did you just say?". Angrily she said, "that damn woman had the nerve to say, Tazhia must've done something to make him mad." What Quan's mother said hurt me because she knew how he really was. My mother told me to get myself and my baby ready to go to the hospital, and I did. After arriving at the hospital and being placed in a room, the police came. They asked questions about what happened, and I had no soft spot to cover anything for him. I also let them know what happened to Quesaan, and before the end of the hospital visit, we both had to get X-rays done. I had to get X-rays on my skull, and my baby had to get X-rays mainly because I fell on him. Everything came back normal and intact for the baby and me. The police gave me a copy of the incident report, and the next morning I took it and went and had a restraining order put on him. Coming back home from taking care of my business, some questions started running through my mind and I just really needed to have a talk with my grandmother. When I got home I asked her, "grandma how did you know to come and get me?" My grandmother said "the Holy Spirit told me to get up and go get Tazhia". I did not call anyone on that morning but it was revealed to my grandmother that I was being held hostage in that apartment. Grandma continued "the Holy Spirit told me who to take with me and how to set everyone up around the apartment." I sat in awe thinking about how amazing it was for God to look out for me the way He does. On this present day I now understand what took place. I followed what God told me to do when I went to the rest room and that was for me to speak out. When I spoke out, my words activated my angels to move on my behalf. Being that my grandmother was the only that can hear God in our home, she received specific instructions on how to get me out of that apartment. Now, what if neither one of us followed the instructions that was given? It could've cost me my life. I was in sync when I didn't even know that I was in sync but overall I am so grateful of my grandmothers anointing, her discernment and obedience.

Two weeks later, I discovered something that had never been spoken of. We went to court for a domestic violence hearing, and after the judge said he was going to charge Quan, his mother stood up, wanting to make a statement. She stood up and told the judge, "Quan is a mental health patient and is in counseling and taking medication. Shocked to my soul, I stood there with my mouth dropped open. I just couldn't believe that no one bothered to mention that this man was dealing with mental illnesses, which ultimately means he was dealing with demonic spirits. Then I thought to myself, this is why he always had appointments to go to. A month had passed and I started getting calls from Quan trying to reconcile the relationship once again. Because I wasn't budging, he then began to say that he would kill himself if I didn't come back to him. My response was, "well, you mind as well go ahead and kill yourself then because I'm not about to let you kill me." I was not taking the baby to him or anything for about two or three months. Quan could not see the Quesaan without his mother or sister accompanying him. Nevertheless, that was the end for me, and I was grateful to God that my baby and I were still alive and well. I enrolled in the community college and started going out and having fun as I moved on with my life.

CHAPTER 7

Covered

After I had come out of everything I went through, I decided to enjoy my life and have fun. Granted, God has been showing and proving himself to me, and I am grateful that he kept me. However, my mind frame at the time was that I wanted to live and do me. So, I enrolled in the community college and started focusing on my future, being a mother, and having fun while doing it. I started going out to parties and clubs just about every weekend. However, God kept and protected me despite my ignorance and lack of understanding about purpose.

One night my friend Shauni and I went to a local club to have a little fun. As we were dancing to ourselves in the corner of the dance floor, we noticed some guys we went to school with. The guys we knew from school were with others we did not know, but they all made a large group. We ended up beside the group of guys as everyone was dancing and having a good time on the dance floor. One of the guys was trying to talk to my friend, and one came and introduced himself to me. We were talking and dancing, and about thirty minutes later, a fight broke out between the guys we were with and some other guys in the club. The club was so packed that it was almost nowhere to run quick enough, so Shauni and I just ran and hid behind the giant speakers. We stayed there until the fight died, and most people were outside. When we left the club and went out, everyone was standing around, and things seemed back to normal with no arguments and no fighting. The two guys talking to Shauni and me came over to us and wanted to meet up at the waffle house. Before the conversation ended, gunshots began to go off. Everyone, including us, started running around in the parking lot, running for safety. Shauni jumped in on the driver's side, and I was on the passenger's side. We both jumped in the car with our heads ducking down, trying to make our way out of the parking lot. When we left the parking lot onto the main street, a car was swerving in front of us. We thought the car was just trying to get away like the rest of us without knowing the situation had worsened. I noticed that when the vehicle in front of us swerved again, its passenger door opened, and someone's body was coming out of the car. I saw the driver leaning over and trying to keep the person from falling out of the vehicle as it swerved across the road. I looked at Shauni and said, "Did you see that? someone's body was falling out of the car". Shauni looked at me and replied, "are you serious?" We pulled over for a minute to think a little because we were curious about who was the person that was hit. So Shauni and I decided to go to the hospital, and when we arrived, we noticed a few guys outside with white tee shirts. My eyes were targeted on the white tee shirts, then I saw some white tees with blood on them. I just sat in silence and prayed for whoever the person's life was. We didn't want to go inside because there were so many people, so we stayed in the car. We heard someone talking about what happened and overheard the person's name. It turns out it was the guy talking to Shauni the whole night. We were both shocked, and all Shauni kept saying was, "oh my God, I can't believe that boy just got shot." She was focused on the fact that this was somebody just talking to her. I was focused on the fact that he and his friend were talking to us when the shots started going off. I kept my thoughts to myself as we began to head back to the house.

When I got home, I couldn't rest at all. The night kept replaying in my head, but the highlight was that God protected us because that bullet that hit him could've hit Shauni or me. Even though this man was fighting for his life, and I was praying for God to spare him and his soul, I just had to thank God that I made it back home to my baby. I eventually fell asleep in the wee hours of the morning, but when I woke up, I found out that He did not make it. I was told that he flatlined

Kept In All Thy Ways   *73*

two times and came back, but the third time, he didn't come back through. Lord knows I was so hurt that someone had to bury their child. Despite that tragedy, I was thankful that not one bullet hit me; I was grateful for how God covered me and allowed me to return home to my baby.

There was another time Shauni and I went out, and on this particular night, we picked up two other friends and met up with our other home girls at the club. About five of us were together that night, having a good time. Again, as usual, we saw people we knew from school, but the main one that stood out to me was Cory. In school, Cory and I were cool, even more like clowns. I remember having math and economics classes together. However, we got kicked out of the math classroom because we always laughed at something.

Moreover, when I saw him at the club, I walked up and said, "hey Cory, how are you?" "What's up, Tay?" I have been doing good; how have you been?" he asked. I told him I was doing well and asked him who had come with him. "I came by myself because I didn't come to stay long. I'm going to stay for a few minutes, and then I'm leaving," Cory said. My friends and I had already been at the club for about two hours before Cory came in, so when he said he would stay for a little while, I told him we would be leaving shortly. About another thirty minutes went by, and I asked the girls if they were ready to go. They weren't ready to go yet, so I waited around to give them more time. I just sat on the pool table watching them, and Cory walked over to the table, and we just sat there and talked for a while about whatever we had going on in our lives. Another fifteen minutes passed, and Cory said he was about to leave. I told him that I was coming out right behind him. So I went and rounded the girls up, and we went on our way towards the car. The girls being who they are, silly and goofing around, stalled us for about another five to seven minutes before we pulled off.

Finally, as we started heading down the street, we saw the traffic barely moving. I was getting impatient because I was ready to get home and bed. As the traffic slowly moved ahead, from a distance, I noticed a red-orange glare. When we got even closer, it was plain and clear that it was a car blazing against a tree. The car was leaning against the tree, meaning the trunk was downward facing the ground, and the front was upward facing the sky. I tried to get as much detail as possible from the car but couldn't determine its make or color. Passing through, my heart went out to whomever the person was, and I just began to pray for their soul. It was still silence in the car for about ten minutes. Then Shauni asked, "Why does someone die every time we go out?" We can't ever go somewhere, have a good time, and just go back home without something happening". I couldn't respond to what she was saying even though I felt the same way. After I dropped my passengers off, I bought something to eat, went straight home, showered, and got in bed.

About twenty to thirty minutes into my sleep, the phone rang. One of my friends asked, "are you asleep?" "I just went to sleep girl; what's up?" I asked tiredly. She said, "you know who was in the car that caught fire?" "Who? I asked as I embraced my heart for what she was about to say". She continued and said, "that was Cory." I sat up in my bed and responded, "say what now?". She repeated herself again and said, "one of his tires had blown out, and he lost control of his car." I sat in silence, thinking I was just talking to him. We were talking about leaving at the same time. I thought, what if the girls weren't goofing off before we got into the car. I thought, what would've happened if we were right behind him? Anything could have happened if we were right behind him, anything. I was grieved, tried to make sense of it, and had difficulty going back to sleep. I stayed up for a little while talking to God and praying. I prayed that his soul would be at peace, and I also thanked God for keeping us. I spoke to God until I drifted back off to sleep.

I stayed away from the club scene for about a year, but I slowly started going back out. One night, my homegirl Shauni and I went out to another club in the same city where we were from. On the way, walking into the club, I heard someone call my name. When I looked back to see who it was, it was an ex-co-worker with whom I had lost contact. He walked over to where I was and reached out for a hug. "Tay, how have you been?" Mitch asked. I replied, "I am doing fine; what about you?". He said, "I can't complain; it was good seeing you again." Make sure you come and holla at me before you leave; I'll be right out here." I said, "Okay, I'll come to see you before I go." Shauni and I continued to walk inside. Once we got inside, we went to the bar and posted at the bar closest to the dance floor. As usual, we saw people we knew because this was our hometown. We sipped our drinks and danced in our little corner away from the crowd. About thirty to forty minutes later, a fight broke out. I said to Shauni, "here goes the foolishness." Next, a dude we knew by the name of Man Man came running to where we were and asked me to hold his chains. I reached my hands out to get his jewelry, and when he turned around, the fight was right where we were. I grabbed Shauni's hand and told her that we were leaving. The club wasn't packed, making it easy for us to make our way to the door. When we stepped outside halfway into the parking lot, gunshot's started going off. We were almost to my car, and instead of Shauni running towards the car, she let go of my hand and ran all the way back to the building. I ran towards my car, and when I got in, I turned it on quickly and backed the car up behind the building. I couldn't leave my best friend, so while I waited for everything to die down, I changed from my skirt and heels to sweatpants and sneakers. When I thought enough time had gone by, I went back to get Shauni.

As I pulled up to the front side of the building, I noticed two people were shot on the ground. One was responsive, and one was not, but my concern was Shauni, so I headed back into the building to look for her. When I approached the front door, Mitch was lying by the door, shot to death. I couldn't believe what I just saw, but at the same time, I didn't have time to sit there and start panicking because I had to make sure my friend was okay. When I got back into the building, I went to the lady's restroom, and in there was where she was hiding. I grabbed her and asked her if she was okay, and she just nodded yes. So, I said, "we have to go. It's two people shot outside". Her response was, "what?" I didn't have the patience to sit and talk. We just needed to be out of the way.

As we went outside, she saw Mitch's body by the door. "Oh my God, Tazhia, you were just talking to him," Shauni said in shock. I felt horrible that someone I knew had just lost their life, but I couldn't operate off of emotions at that moment. Somebody out of the two of us had to think clearly. Once we got back into the car, we drove off the premises for about thirty minutes, but I wanted to go back and make sure there was somebody out there to pick up Mitch's body. The other guy was still living and was rushed to the hospital. Most of the people had left, and I was still wondering why no one had come to pick Mitch up yet. Why wasn't he covered up? I couldn't break down in tears, I don't know why, but I was getting upset that Mitch was just left the way he was. Suddenly, Man Man came up to the car from out of nowhere, asking if he could drop him off. I don't know what happened to his ride, but Man Man was a part of the fight that broke out before the shooting began.

Because I knew Man Man well and wanted him to get home safely, I gave him a ride home. He broke down and flipped out on the way to his house. Man Man and Mitch were friends, and he wanted revenge. He knew who was a part of the fight and shooting even though he didn't see every detail of what took place outside because he was inside. Shauni and I tried our best to talk sense into Man Man to keep him from going over the edge. When I pulled up to his destination, he told me to wait because he was going to get his gun. When he entered the house, I pulled off because I wasn't trying to be involved with another person getting shot or killed.

Before returning to my place, I went back to the club to see if anyone had picked up Mitch's body. It was about 5:30 am and not much longer before the sun rose, and he was still lying there. I couldn't even cry, but I was more upset because I was tired of people losing their lives for nothing. Shauni and I got to my place, and she stayed in my son's room to rest. I couldn't rest at all; I was up just thinking about everything. Thinking about his soul, his children, and his family. I wondered what transitions he went through when he left his human body. I was thinking about what he could be seeing or feeling. I don't know when I finally drifted off to sleep, but I knew the sun was shining and the birds were chirping. Again, all I could do was thank God that he kept Shauni and me once again. This time things were different. The club thing scene had really put a bad taste in my mouth, and I just fell back from the club scene. The desire and the fun of it were snatched away from me. With all that I was around to see, I honestly wondered why God was sparing my life. I felt like I cheated death many times and started questioning God about me. Why was I in places with close contact with those that lost their lives, but I still was here? God was beginning to get my attention, and even though I couldn't fully understand and still made errors, I knew God was keeping me for a reason. I had to begin searching to find out the answers to why He kept me through so much.

CHAPTER 8

Second Time Around

Five years later, I repeated the same cycle as most young black women my age. I was twenty-three with two children by two different fathers and was not with either of them. I was upset with myself because I had always seen my life as being different from what it actually was. However, I never got comfortable and complacent; I wanted more because I felt there was more to me despite my circumstances.

What happened between Rashad and me was a different experience. I simply walked away due to deception, drama, and confusion. He led me to think that he had moved on from his relationship with his ex, but he was going back and forth between us. I was being told one thing while the other woman was being told something different. As time passed, the truth started coming out from the people he was always around.

Furthermore, it's been times when she saw us together, and she never approached him. She always came at me with hostility, ready to fight. When I asked him what was happening and why this woman was behaving the way she was, he would say, "that's how she is." He would also say she is jealous because I don't want her no more, or he'll just say something is wrong with her.

One night, Rashad and I went to a local sports bar with his family and friends to play pool and have drinks. I started hearing whispers of this woman being on her way from his siblings. He came to me saying that we needed to leave. I asked him, "why do we need to leave from where were because she is coming?" The second question I had was, how did she even know where we were at? He walked off but returned, repeating, "we needed to leave." Because I wanted to get to the bottom of it, I told him I was not running from nobody. He seemed to have gotten agitated, and he left. About fifteen minutes later, this woman shows up with about ten to fifteen people with her to jump me. Did he know her plans concerning me when he chose to leave? I don't know. However, what both of us did know was that I was a few weeks pregnant. Everything I felt was confirmed when he walked out of the door. I couldn't look at him the same way, especially since I was pregnant with his child. I couldn't respect a man who ran from taking accountability, the responsibility of protecting, or standing up for me. That was it; he showed his true colors earlier than expected, and that cowardly move put the icing on the cake for me.

When Rashad left me at that sports bar with his people, some were upset about the situation and how he chose to handle it. They did not know I was pregnant, but his sister, Jazz, picked up on it because we were around one another often. Furthermore, she looked at me and said, "don't worry about them; I'm not going to let anything happen to you; I know you got my niece or nephew in there." I know she meant well, but if all of them wanted to jump on me, they could've at any given time, and she wouldn't have been able to do much about it.

Nevertheless, with all the loud music, smoking, drinking, and foul language, I managed to tap deep within my spirit and didn't realize it. I prayed inwardly, "Lord, protect and cover me; please don't allow anything to happen to make me lose my baby." I did not fully understand who I was and what God placed inside of me back then, but I started testing it out even more when I realized when I said something, it happened. When I felt strongly about something, that's what it was. Even specific thoughts and dreams I had came to pass. I didn't have an understanding of tapping or operating in the spirit. I learned from my past experiences to follow what I felt strongly about. Still, it's something that just was a part of me, that I was born with.

I held on to my peace, composure, and confidence in what I had just asked the Lord and showed no fear in that place. I walked around alone with this woman and her clique following me everywhere. I even went to the lady's restroom all by myself, and they also followed me there. In the lady's room, I stood in line waiting for someone to come out of the stall, and they all walked in, standing right behind me. The ex, who really came for me, stepped from behind and stood beside me. I smiled at her because it was funny to me that she was so angry and was making all kinds of faces while huffing and puffing but couldn't put not one finger on me. I went inside the stall, and his sister came in and knocked on the door to let me know she was there. When I came out of the stall, I went to get some water from the bar, and they were still following me. She started hollering and cussing over the music; I looked back at her to let her know I had heard her. However, I took my time and walked over to where the rest of Rashad's friends and family were, and I let them know that I was leaving to go home. His sister said, "well, I'll walk you outside." When we got outside, I noticed that this woman had her mother and some other older women standing outside waiting.

I shook my head at how foolish they looked, posted up in the parking lot when they knew they needed to be home in bed somewhere. Rashad's ex came out of the place cussing and telling me what she would do to me, trying to show off for her people. I ignored her and said goodbye to Jazz as she stayed near the front door. I turned to look at the minions one last time and walked to my car. Jazz remained near the door, and no matter how angry Rashad's ex sounded and how much she cussed, she didn't flinch, and nobody else did either. I know it had nothing to do with his sister, but because I had holy ones around me who were keeping and protecting me. They couldn't lay a finger on me when I knew they really wanted to. I am not bragging, but I boast in the Lord because I now understand how He kept me.

However, that night was the last night of my dealing with him. When I walked away from the mess, everyone I ran into who knew him was saying he was back with her. I was so unbothered that I couldn't care less about what they had going on. I prepared myself mentally, emotionally, and physically to take care of my responsibility on my own. I worked until I was a little over eight months, and I prepared everything for the birth of my baby without asking or looking for him to do anything.

One day my mucus plug came down, and I thought this baby was coming quickly since I was active my whole pregnancy. Unfortunately, for two days, I was contracting but was not dilating. When I arrived at my doctor's office on the third day, the doctor told me that I wasn't dilating. "Do you want to try on your own, or do you want to do the cesarean?" asked the doctor. I was still having contractions as he checked me, so I told him I'd go with the cesarean because I just wanted the contractions to stop. "Did you eat or drink anything yet?" he asked. "No, I'm hurting too much to eat or drink."

Moreover, he called the hospital to tell them I was on my way for delivery. When he hung up, he told me to go to the hospital at 1pm, and they would admit me. It was already after 12pm, so I just went to the hospital and sent my cousin that I had with me to get my bags from the house. Meanwhile, I was admitted to the hospital and started making phone calls to let my family know I was admitted and about to go into delivery. I know it was last minute. My mother was at work, my grandmother was busy, and I never picked up the phone to call anyone on the baby's father's side of the family. I prayed that everything would be smooth and went into that operating room alone.

The anesthesiologist came in to start the epidural and asked me to sit up on the table with my pillow bent over as much as I could. I kept feeling this person sticking, sticking, and sticking. So I yelled out, "what are you doing?" I was already having contractions on top of it. The anesthesiologist said I'm trying to get the epidural in the right spot. I yelled again, "just hurry up, please." When I was laid down on the table, all I knew was that shortly afterward, breathing became very difficult. I was trying to let the nurse know that I couldn't breathe, and I suddenly passed out. I don't remember what was happening other than that. They just told me that I had stopped breathing altogether. I was forced to go under general anesthesia because something was going on with the epidural that was never explained to me. My guess was there was too much epidural in my system because even the regular amount of epidural is heavy on a person breathing. However, I was put to sleep and woke up in recovery. I couldn't see my baby immediately because they had a hard time with him. When my mother got to the hospital, they told her my baby wasn't responding. My guess would be that I had too much epidural in my system, which affected my baby too. I just thank God for keeping my baby and me because anything could've happened.

During my hospital stay, the only person that reached out to me was his sister. I did not run behind anyone like a bitter baby mother trying to be messy or vengeful. I did what I had to do and assumed the position I had to fill. I got some of my ways from my mother because she was always a woman who did what she needed to provide so that we would have everything. I stepped into the role just like that because it was so much mess going on before anything real could get started, and I thank God for giving me the peace to walk away.

CHAPTER 9

Influences

After going through the last disastrous relationship, you would think I would just be tired of men and the foolery that came along with them. With all the hurt and disappointment that I experienced, I should've given up on love and just stayed to myself until I was sure that God sent me the right man. But because of the lack of wisdom and the lack of someone being in my life to give me wisdom, I took another chance at love with the wrong man once again. I still had love in my heart to give not knowing that was the area of my heart that belonged to God. The void that was in my heart I was trying to satisfy and fulfill did not belong to any man because man is incapable of filling areas that only belong to God. I gave it another chance and this time, it cost me some things.

The next relationship that I was in I really thought was going to work. I thought it was going to work between Rick and I mainly because I knew his mother Robin. All three of us worked at the same place and I really hadn't noticed him until he came to the area where Robin and I worked to talk to his mother. After he left to go back to his department, she said "Tazhia, my son needs a nice girl like you in his life". From that moment Robin was putting in word both ways, with me as well as with her son to make sure we would give it a try between us.

Months went by with us dealing with one another and everything was good. Rick and I were spending a lot of time getting to know one another and he started taking me around to some of the neighborhood spots where he hung out to meet some of his friends. Eventually, things were getting pretty serious with us and he started taking me around his family. I loved everything about him, especially the fact that he was family oriented. Rick had no problem with accepting my two boys and his family didn't either.

About a year into it, Rick eventually moved in with me in my place. Things were smooth and he was a good help to me with the kids and with things around the house. We took turns cooking dinner, going shopping, and even cleaning. It was a relief to me because I appreciated the extra help especially with my boys and with the bills. Whenever we talked, there was understanding and he became my best friend. Going out clubbing the way I used to was no longer what I enjoyed doing because something was always happening to someone so sitting home or going to family functions on the weekends with Rick and the kids was fine with me. Apart from this, sometimes we traveled and stayed out of town with the kids and sometimes we took them to my mother's house for the weekends. If we did go out to a club, it was a small intimate setting where it would be mainly people that he grew up with and some family. I enjoyed everything and I was falling more and more in love with him everyday.

One day, I just started noticing little things that maybe I haven't been paying attention to before. I knew sometimes he wanted to hang out with his coworkers after work but I never was on his back about it because I looked at it like that was just time he wanted to be with his friends. Two to three days a week he would stay out with them at the corner store for about two or three hours and about the time he comes home I would have dinner started so it wasn't a big deal to me. It started to become a problem on one Valentine's Day weekend. We planned to go away for the weekend beginning on that Friday after work. Rick called me and told me that he was going to play cards for a little while and then he was coming home so we could leave. Four, five, and six hours went by and there was not a phone call from him and when I called, he didn't answer the phone.

Our bags were packed and were by the door the night before so we wouldn't have much to do when it was time to leave, however, I fell asleep on the sofa right across from the door waiting for him to walk in. All of a sudden, seven o'clock the next morning, Rick came into the house stumbling over the bags that were by the door. I sat up and looked at him, and didn't say anything because he was drunk. He looked at me and said "I know you are mad, I'm sorry, I messed up" then he walked off. I didn't utter a single word. Rick made his way to the room and just laid on the floor on his side of the bed. It came back to me that he mentioned something about one of the guys having a card game so I waited until I knew he was deep in his sleep and I went straight to his pockets to check his wallet.

When I opened his wallet, there was nothing in there but a one hundred dollar bill. I was so upset and disappointed because I knew he just got paid and he blew his whole check playing cards. We couldn't go anywhere if we wanted to because I used my check to pay for the utility bills and his check was supposed to be for our weekend. Rick's cousin Meranda, whom I became friends with, called and asked if we were still going to meet them. I told her no because he had been out all night playing cards, came home drunk, and passed out. I found out this was the kind of stuff he used to do before he moved in with me. I guess he was trying to do away with it since he was in a new relationship but complacency began to settle in.

Whenever he knew I was upset with him, he wouldn't hang out or drink. He would come home after work and wouldn't really answer the phone when his friends began to call him to come hang out. In spite of this, as his friends began to pick at him, by calling him names such as: whipped and a sucker, Rick started to feel that he had to prove a point to them as if they were kids in high school. The more they said negative things to him, the more he began to sway. He then started staying at the store with the guys everyday after work drinking, playing dice, buying scratch offs or either going to one of their houses to play cards. The only time he didn't stay out with them was on Saturdays and Sundays. This was a habit that was now becoming selfish, inconsiderate, and disrespectful.

His behavior became selfish and inconsiderate because these men became such a voice of influence to him that he didn't give second thoughts of how this would affect his home. All of which was bringing disrespect to me and our relationship. I would say something about the disrespect of him coming and going as he felt without considering me and it would go nowhere. Some nights when he would come in drunk, I will deliberately look in his phone after he passes out. They say that when you go searching, you get just what you asked for. I didn't mind and didn't care as long as I found out what I needed to know. Unsurprisingly, I found just what I thought. Not only was he hanging out drinking and gambling, he was also in contact with two other women. One was another woman from the job and the other was a classmate that he went to school with. After I told him how I felt about everything and the mess still continued, I stopped talking. I stopped the nagging and complaining and I put my focus on me. I was stacking and saving my money, yet, I stopped sitting around the house waiting for him to come home. I started getting myself dressed and taking myself out. I completely blocked out what was going on with him because in my mind I was preparing myself for however the chips may have fallen.

Two wrongs don't make it right but I decided to give Rick a taste of his medicine. I wasn't thinking spiritually because I wasn't in that mind set so I gave him what he gave me. The plant that we all was working at was doing some laying off and moving others around, unfortunately I was moved right in the same department as Rick and on the same production line. I was at the beginning of the line and he was at the end of the line, in which the line was about a block long. There was a guy that I worked with that had interest in me named Don. He watched and listened to everything that was going on and knew about everything. He listened to how the guys at work talked about Rick being a punk and always wanting to run home like he was running home to his momma. He heard and he sat quietly on it.

One day Don approached me saying "that's messed up how ole boy is doing you". He continued and said "I think you are a good woman and I bet all of those fools that's saying that stuff about him are probably jealous". I looked at him somewhat baffled and said " people are talking like that huh? It was crazy to me how the very people that were supposed to be friends of Rick's, were talking about him to other people. I was feeding Rick the silent treatment because he didn't care about how I felt so I let people say whatever about him without defending him. Don and I started talking more, and eventually we exchanged numbers. People at the job began noticing that I wasn't pressed about Rick and that I was enjoying conversation with Don; so as people normally would, they assumed I was sleeping with Don. Which was inaccurate but I let people say whatever they wanted to say. After sitting in the house hurt and wasting tears when the person that I loved didn't love me back enough to see what was happening, I decided to go out with Don a few times. I didn't think about everything thoroughly and how it would turn out, I just was a young woman in my mid-twenties that was reacting. What I should've did, was leave Rick and that house to start over but I think somewhere deep down inside of me was hoping that everything would get back on track but it didn't.

When some people get complacent in a relationship, they tend to mistreat and take advantage of the ones that love them. On the other hand, when the mistreated stop paying any attention to the complacent, the complacent is now paying attention to why they aren't being paid attention to anymore. This is what Rick started doing. He was hearing about how Don always came to talk to me and checked on me. One day Rick walked over to my work area and saw Don bringing me something to drink. All of a sudden Rick cared so much when we basically were living like roommates because he was doing his own thing. He came to my work area like he just busted me, trying to get loud, and I just looked at him. I didn't respond because he was trying to make a scene and besides, he didn't care about anything concerning me all before. From that day, he started paying attention to everything that I did and wherever I decided to go. He even said he was going to have a private eye watching me. It wasn't that serious to me like how Rick was making it because Don understood me and where I was coming from.

I don't know what side of the bed Rick woke up on one Saturday, but he got up and cooked breakfast and wanted to talk. Rick started by saying "I apologize for all the changes that we are going through and I apologize for how I have been treating you". I sat and I just listened to everything that he wanted to get off of his chest. He asked me if I slept with Don and my answer was no. I asked him about the women that he was in contact with and he said it meant nothing to him. Rick admitted that he was too focused on proving a point to the guys that he was still the same Rick. Nonetheless, at the end of our conversation he asked if we can start over with a clean slate. I told him that I needed to think about it but eventually I agreed.

Rick and I changed our cell numbers and took some time off of work to block all the distractions out to focus on us. Things were getting back on the right track and it felt like we rekindled what we had at the beginning of our relationship. When we got back to work, everyone was looking at us so puzzled because we were getting along. He was doing his part again, checking on me, sending food or drinks to me that he brought, and some days we had lunch together. I can tell that people were trying to figure out what we had going on and that they were more excited to see us not getting along. Even the ones that was close to him like his so called friends and a few family members.

Instead of encouraging love and happiness they always discouraged him and talked about me. With our new start and us forgiving one another, Rick never stood up to them and defended me. I thought I loved everything about him until I saw how weak he was when it came to outside influences. He had no positive people in his corner to build him up and to encourage him as a man. Not even his cousin Meranda that I thought was cool with me. She was married just like some of his friends were but all of them, including her, were living double lives and had other partners other than their spouse.

About two months went by since our clean slate and the job laid some people off and sent some to other departments. I was one of them that was sent to another department until my department picked back up again. I was happy to get out of that department from all those messy people. I felt like I could breathe again and Rick and I started thinking about having a baby (if only my today self would've been able to talk to past self, I would've denied that thought real quick; but again I didn't have the wisdom that I have today). We wanted to take our relationship to another level so the talk of marriage and a baby was on the table. Surprisingly, the next month my cycle was late. Due to pulling overtime hours at work and just getting tired of hearing childish stuff from people that were supposed to be older than me, I took my mind off of having a baby.

Needless to say, I was at work one day and I began to feel so irritable and sick. I was trying to deal with it for hours but I went to my team leader, who happened to be my uncle's girlfriend, and told her I think I'm getting sick. I asked her if I could go home cause I felt weak and I just needed to go get in the bed. She looked at me and said "what's wrong? Are you pregnant?" My answer was "no girl" and she just told me to go ahead and clock out and go home and get some rest. When I walked away, I pulled my phone out to look at the date and I realized that my cycle was late. Then I texted Rick and told him that I was going home because I didn't feel well and I did just that. I didn't stop anywhere excitedly to get a test because I had no strength for that. I felt sick as a dog so I went home and slept until Rick called me when he got off from work. He called to check on me and didn't mention anything to him until I knew for sure if I was pregnant or not. When we got off the phone I got out of the bed, showered, and went to the store to get a test.

On that day Rick said he was going by the store for a few minutes so he did not come straight home. I went to get a few ept tests and came back home to put dinner on the stove. I couldn't wait for him to come home so I took the test without him and just like that, the test was positive. I called Rick and asked him when he was going to be on the way to the house because I needed to tell him something. He asked "what is it?" I told him "I don't know if I need to say it now because you are around other people" He said "it's ok, you can tell me". All I said was "I just took a pregnancy test" and excitedly he said "and it was positive?" I said yes. He yelled out "yes". The guys in the background started asking "what happened". Through the tone in his voice, I could tell he had a big smile on his face as he told them "she's pregnant". I could hear the reactions from everyone in the background "she's pregnant? Congratulations". He was excited because in his mind it was going to be a boy.

My first prenatal appointment was about a month later but they referred me to the hospital to get a transvaginal ultrasound because my HCG levels weren't elevating and matching with how many weeks I was. The ultrasound tech told me that in some cases, it could possibly mean that the embryo wasn't growing and with time it could eventually dissolve and I'll lose the baby. The tech also told me that she was going to send the ultrasound results back to my doctor and the best thing to do was to wait a few weeks later to see if there has been a change in the hormone levels and do another ultrasound, so another appointment was scheduled with my OB doctor about two weeks later. When I left the hospital, I was somewhat sad but I was hopeful at the same time. I called my grandmother and told her what was happening. My grandmother listened to everything that I said and before we got off the phone she said "not so, there's nothing wrong with your pregnancy". She prayed and told me not to worry myself and to get plenty of rest. With her being a christian all of her life, she didn't judge me. She was loving and supportive towards me.

The next day Meranda stopped by my house to bring something to Rick and I heard her in the living room asking "where is Tazhia?" He said "she's in the room lying down". So Meranda makes her way to my bedroom to come check on me. She asked how I was feeling and then asked how many weeks I was. I went on to tell her the situation that was going on and she showed concern and offered to come with me to the doctor on my next visit. I took her up on her offer and told her that it would be nice if she came with me. We talked more than before because we came to find out she was pregnant too. She was six weeks ahead of me and we basically became pregnant buddies. I put aside the things that I knew she said about me because I understood that me and Rick were going through a lot and she was his cousin so if anything she was reacting as any other family member would. Moving forward, two weeks later Meranda goes with Rick and I to the doctor for support. We were so relieved to find out that the baby was growing and everything was fine. We just needed to give it a little time because it was early in the pregnancy. Rick called his mother and let her know that the baby was fine and I called my grandmother and told her the same news. I didn't tell anyone besides my grandmother in my family that I was pregnant until I got into my second trimester. We were excited and felt blessed that God saw fit to let us have a normal pregnancy. Everything was fine between us until Rick started hanging out at the store again.

CHAPTER 10

The Breaking

"Here comes the foolery again," I said to Rick. He started to hang out at the store again after work. Little by little and day by day, I started seeing the same foolishness circling back around. Rick began to come home telling me how these same people were again saying stuff, trying to be funny. I screamed, "Oh my God, trying to be funny about what?" He said they were trying to be jokey by saying the baby might not be his. I was four months pregnant when all of this about the baby started kicking up.

I became highly agitated with Rick and started telling him off. "How in the hell are you feeling some kind of way and bothered by what someone else is saying? You act as if you didn't know what you were doing or like we never had this conversation". "What kind of friends is that to always be pumping you up with negativity? They are not your friends" Rick couldn't say anything back. I was so frustrated I walked into the bedroom and slammed the door.

Consequently, he started staying at the store every day after work. The more he stayed after work, the more distant we became. He went back to playing card games, money was becoming an issue, and he wasn't paying his portion of the bills, which was the rent. I paid the utilities and found myself taking money that I was saving for the baby and had been paying the rent too. It would've been different if I were on my own. There's no way I would've been okay with Rick running in and out without handling his responsibilities.

However, I waited to see if he would jump back in the swing of things or if I needed to leave. I paid the rent for the past two months, which was rent time again. I thought about it, and even though I didn't want to go through that moving process, I would move back home, save money, and start over with my children. I gave Rick as much time as possible to get it right, but I had to leave when Rick didn't have the money for rent the third time. If the rent wasn't paid by the fifth of each month, there would be a ten-dollar daily fee beginning on the sixth day. If there was an eviction filing by the fifteenth, the processing fee was an extra forty dollars.

As much as I was agitated with the situation, I tried to give Rick the benefit of the doubt. So, I got in my truck and headed to the store. When I got there, one of Rick's homeboys came to speak to me, but Rick never came to see what I wanted. I told Rick's friend to tell him that I needed to talk to him. I waited on him for about fifteen minutes, but Rick never came to see what I wanted. I didn't know what his issue was with me; maybe he was ashamed since there was so much chatter about me. After just sitting and waiting, I left, and Rick never called or came home when he knew it was rent time.

I was livid. I was so tired of the stupidity that was going on and being with a man with no backbone. I went home and packed everything that I could into my truck, and by the time I was finished, I still hadn't heard anything from Rick. When I packed, I made sure I left nothing for him to be comfortable in the house. I took the linen and pillows off the bed and everything out of the linen closet. I took all the wash rags, towels, and the other comforter sets. I admit I was petty about it and even took the television too. The only thing I left was the furniture, the dishes, some food, and a note saying I was coming back to clear out the rest of my stuff.

I called my mother to tell her that I had packed my stuff and was coming home. On the route that took me to my mother's house, I had no choice but to go past the store where the guys were standing. I didn't know if he saw me, and I didn't care. When I got to my mother's house, I showered, lay down, and then Rick started calling my phone. I knew he had made it to the house and saw that I left him for him to start calling me, but just like he ignored me, I ignored him until I was ready to talk. I did not communicate with Rick for about three days. When I spoke to him again, he moved back to his mother's house. I didn't know how he got there, and I didn't ask. He was crying, saying he was sorry for hurting me and being a screwup. He also told me that he never thought I would leave him. As much as he was pouring his heart out, something in me wouldn't allow me to feel pushed to go back. I no longer trusted or felt secure with him being the man of my life.

I put my things in storage and went to stay with my uncle and his wife. It was more room at their house, so I stayed there for the remainder of my pregnancy. I continued working, and Rick and I acted as if nothing had happened around people even though we were going to separate homes. We ate together on our breaks, and he checked on me constantly. I knew deep down that a part of him was happy to be back at his mother's house, mainly so he wouldn't have to answer anyone about anything. He was just trying to be respectful towards me because now the guys were talking about him not being man enough to take care of his home. Still, in my eyes, none of them are considered real friends.

I worked until I was eight and a half months pregnant. Standing up on concrete floors for eight to ten hours every day was beginning to get painful, so I went on maternity leave a little early. The baby was weighing down on my sciatica nerve and causing sharp pain in my legs and lower back. However, I continued getting things together for my baby while on leave. Rick was just giving me money here and there to buy stuff; it wasn't too much to brag about. Some days, Rick and I did things together, and other days he didn't answer the phone or show up. I tried not to focus on other things, but I felt something else was going on with him. Despite whatever he told me, I kept my eyes focused on what I needed to do. I went into nesting mode, and that's what my total focus was on, preparing myself and my other children for the new arrival.

My OB doctor had to schedule me for a cesarean because it's required after I had two. The day before my appointment, I told Rick to come and get my truck before he went to work so we could go to the hospital together when he got off. His new shift was from 6pm to 4am, so he had to come and get me because we had to be at the hospital and checked in by 5:30am. I had me and the baby bags packed by the door from the night before. When I got up, I showered, got dressed, and was ready by 4:40am. Rick did not get to the house till about 5:00am. When he came into the house to help me load the truck, he was reeking of alcohol. As soon as I smelled him, I said, "please tell me you are not drunk?" He responded, "no, I just had a few shots with the fellas to celebrate ."I didn't say anything else; I kept walking with my bag to the truck.

We arrived at the hospital in time, and I checked in at the nurses' station. Once I checked in, they put me in my room to start the paperwork and to get me set up. My little sister was there as well to support and help me. Rick went back and forth in the room because his nerves were getting the best of him. The nurse started the IV, set the catheter in place, and did some blood work just in case I needed a blood transfusion. The nurse also asked me if I wanted to opt out, and I thought that was a good idea since so many people were worrying if my baby belonged to Rick. I only wanted people that I was close with to be able to contact me through the hospital. If I didn't give them the information myself, they wouldn't have access to the room or my room number.

Moving forward, the nurses unlocked the bed's wheels and grabbed the IV pole, and we started rolling to the operating room. I didn't know if Rick was tired from working or drunk, but he was in the waiting room with his scrubs on sleep. My sister stood in his place with me in the operating room. Right before they started the incision, the nurse told me my mother wanted to come into the room with me. Maybe because she saw Rick sleeping in the waiting room when she got to the hospital. I didn't know what was happening to him, but I was strapped to the bed with the oxygen tube in my nose. The blue sheets were up and ready to start the procedure. My mother and sister went back and forth about who would be in the room. The nurse asked, "Ms. Hamilton, who do you want to be in here with you?" I told her, "it doesn't matter." I felt like if it wasn't the father of my child; I didn't even care. So my little sister got irritated because she really wanted to be with me but got up and let our mother take her place.

Once they started the incision, that was it. No one could come in or leave out until the procedure was done. Furthermore, about ten to fifteen minutes later, I heard the nurse say, "congratulations, it's a boy." Then there was a loud cry from such a little human being. My mother looked at the baby, smiling, and said, "he looks like he's over there fighting them." When they bought the baby over to me, they held him close to me so we could be skin-to-skin. I love how babies smell so good and their skin is so soft. I was so ready to have my baby in my arms. Shortly after that, I was wheeled into the recovery room to stay for about thirty minutes to an hour. Rick came to the back where I was to see if everything was okay. I didn't ask him why he wasn't in the operating room with me or anything to that extent. I didn't ask because I didn't care. When my hour was up in the recovery room, they wheeled my bed to where I would be for the rest of my stay. My sister and my mother stayed for a little while, but the two of them left together.

I don't know how long I was in that room before Meranda called my cell phone, and Rick held it to my ear. Meranda asked what room I was in because I opted out. I told her the room number, and she was in my room in less than ten minutes. Even with me still under anesthesia, I was alert and heard everything. Meranda didn't think I was because I didn't feel like responding too much. This woman washed her hands and walked over to my baby while talking to me to see if I was alert enough to hear everything; she then picked my baby up and had the audacity to say to my son's father, "Rick, this is not your baby." Meranda, the one that was my pregnancy buddy, my baby's cousin, and the one that pretended to be my friend. I was blinking and seeing what was happening when they didn't think I was seeing. Like I said, I just didn't say anything. Rick sat there and said, "

Oh, you don't think so." If I had the strength to get off that bed, I would've turned that room upside down, but God allowed me to just lay there to listen to show me who the snake was, the main one stirring up all the confusion. I was hurt as I listened to this woman put the batteries in Rick's back while putting the knife in mine. I remained humble and didn't say a word about it. I couldn't understand her motive and why she pretended to be my friend. I could see if she was not related to Rick and just was a friend of mine that secretly had a thing for him. It made no sense to me, especially since I was genuine to her. Rick said nothing in my defense and just sat there like a weak man. Again, we planned this pregnancy, and he followed everyone's sayings as if he had no clue. Moreover, when the snake in disguise was ready to leave, Rick walked over to me and tapped me to tell me he was going home to get some rest and was coming back later.

Later that afternoon, Rick's mother, Robin, came to the hospital to see the baby and me. I know she had doubts because Meranda talked about me to every person she came into contact with. She added the coal, the lighter fluid, and the match and still went back to throw gasoline on top of the fire. However, Robin undoubtedly held my baby in her arms and said, "this is my grandbaby ."Tears started to flow from my eyes as she continued to say, "this baby looks just like Rick's father and Rick when he was a baby ."She pulled his hat off his head and said, "oh my God, he looks like Rick's grandmother too ."I wiped my eyes and forced out a smile when my heart was really crushed. Not that I needed her reassurance, but it felt good to have not just anybody but my baby's grandmother embrace him as her own. I don't think she understood how much that meant to me.

Furthermore, as she was getting ready to leave, she asked me what I wanted to eat, that she would cook and send the food back with Rick. I told her it didn't matter as long as her macaroni was on the plate, and we laughed as she made her exit. The first twenty-four hours after my cesarean, I had to stay in bed with a catheter and the pumps on my feet to prevent blood clots. I slept as much as possible while it was quiet and had the nurses keep my baby in the nursery the rest of the night because I needed help, and Rick never returned that night. I thought he must've just been tired and was resting because whenever I called his cell phone, I wasn't getting an answer. I spoke with Rick several times the following day about him coming back to the hospital. He never came back until it was time for us to be discharged. I was left to fend for myself the whole stay at the hospital when I could barely move around. I had little help when my family came to the hospital. I didn't want to ask anyone to stay with me because they had their own lives, and I didn't want to ask anyone to go out of their way to help me. I just asked God to give me the strength to do what I needed to for me and my baby while crouched over, dragging, and crying. I kept my mindset on the fact that I wasn't always going to be down and that I would bounce back like every other time. I cried and released when I needed to, but my children were my motivation for the most part. Life dealt me all types of hands, but one thing about me is I take that hand and do what I have to do with it to make it work for me.

CHAPTER 11

The Pressing

Two months later, I moved into my own place just like I said I would. I filed for unemployment before I had the baby and had been saving those checks. I then filed my tax return and paid my car off and whatever I had left I just banked it. Moreover, I moved into my own place to start over and it felt good just to be up on my feet again. Not that I was expecting anything from Rick but everything that I did, I was able to do because I was praying my way through. Rick didn't offer to help with anything, not even a hand to help with his son. I was managing the best way that I could and even though I was not ready to go back to work, I had to. Money was beginning to run out so I made a doctor's appointment to be cleared to go back to work.

Everything was great with my appointment and I already knew what I had to do as far as the children. My oldest two sons, Quesaan and Quansae had to be taken to my mother's house in the mornings for them to get on the bus for school. My newborn Qadir was being taken to an older woman that I knew who cared for children for a living. Quesaan was nine years old and Quansae was four years old at this time. Although getting up extra early was exceptionally exhausting, I was okay with the things I had to do because in my mind everything was about to get back on track. Little did I know, my whole world was about to be turned upside down, again.

My first day back at work was so refreshing to me. I was happy with the thought of being able to provide for my children and myself without having to worry about asking anybody for help. I really haven't been talking to Rick like that simply because he was a people pleaser. Even when we spoke, he would try to be manipulative and play mind games as if he had nothing going on with anybody else and would try to handle me as a random chick instead of his son's mother. I knew he was lying because I knew him as well as I knew the code to his voicemail.

I didn't tell Rick when I was coming back to work but apparently, he got wind from everyone else talking about it when I showed up. Rick walked down to my area like he was coming to check on me and was trying to make small talk like he really cared. As he was talking, I sensed the nervousness in him. I talked as my usual self, smiling, unbothered, and not saying much. Even if there were things that I wanted to say to him, I didn't say them. I simply answered his question or made a short comment on whatever he said. With my experience from working in a manufacturing plant, I know that people are always watching and are always waiting to have something to talk about. Additionally, the people in that environment are so nosey they'll read your lips too. However, I maintained my composure. As the week went on, Rick started sitting with me on our breaks because I sat alone and to myself. He was even bringing me food from home that his mother cooked for me. It seemed as if he wanted to do better unless he just came to the reality that I wasn't going to be pregnant and swollen forever and that I was back to myself. Some days he would even ride back home with me to see Qadir and spend time with the boys. I was trying to be nice to him even though he was undeserving. Besides, I just knew something else was up with him but I couldn't pinpoint it.

One day at work, the production line just so happened to run out of parts and was down for about 45 minutes. For the first 15-20 minutes everyone was cleaning up their workstations and restocking their parts but as soon as I finished, something told me to go walk to the other end of the line. I didn't really want to go. Instead, I sent my friend Mel to go see what Rick was doing since he was like a brother to me. I had a strong gut feeling that something was up with Rick so I told Mel to go see what he was doing without him noticing. My stomach was balling in knots when Mel came back and said "he's down there talking to some chick on the forklift". I looked at him and said "seriously?" His reply was "for real, some dark skin girl with a turquoise shirt on". As soon as he said the shirt color I knew just who he was talking about as everything started coming back to me about this woman. I said to Mel "I'll be right back" and I started walking. Once I made it past the wall that divided the sides of the production line, I saw Rick talking and smiling from ear to ear. When I got to his station he told the woman on the forklift, to leave. I said in the kindest, most polite way to Rick, " oh this is your new friend?" I then said to her "no, you don't have to leave, I'll leave". As I turned around to walk back, it seemed like everyone in the plant was looking at me waiting for a reaction. I kept my composure as I made it back on my end of the line and said to Mel "that's the chick he's seeing, isn't it?" Mel looked at me and said, "that's what they've been saying". I told Mel to look into my eyes and asked "so you mean to tell me, everybody in here knows that Rick has been messing around with this lady knowing I just had a baby with him and nobody said nothing to me about it?" His response was "yeah, I'm sorry you have to deal with that" I chuckled, shook my head, and said, "it's cool". I couldn't say what I really wanted to say because people were watching and whispering to one another. Again, I held my composure and went back to my workstation.

With all the changes Rick took me through, doubting me, accusing me, and neglecting not only me but his son; I felt like I was about to blow a fuse. The thoughts came back to me of when I was in the hospital and how Rick never came back until I was discharged along with the thought of the times that I called and he didn't answer the phone. Suddenly, it hit me. Rick was seeing this woman with my vehicle when I was in the hospital. I went from feeling angry to feeling so hurt, betrayed, and manipulated. God was showing me the truth in everything. Rick was manipulative and put the excuse for his behavior on rumors when all the while it was just a cover of the dirt he was doing. I couldn't believe how people dragged my name in the mud but covered him in his wrong. I was made to look like a bed-hopping whore that was trying to put a baby on him, meanwhile, everyone covered up what was really going on. I was hurt and humiliated down to my soul. My team leader Vet, who was Meranda's first cousin, walked over to my area and said "Tay you better not cry, fix your face".

I asked Vet to relieve me from my station so I can go to the lady's room. She said "Tay hold it together, do not break down in here". No matter what she said, my only response was "can you relieve me please?" Vet knew everything about everything because her cousin stayed with my name in her mouth but at the same time it made her grow closer to me out of compassion. Rick used to say to me, "you better watch Vet, she's not your friend". I knew that she was around when they talked about me but I also figured out how manipulative he could be. He knew that she knew about his dirty deeds, but I also figured out that he was trying to draw a wedge so that I wouldn't find out anything from her. I understood that she did not want to get caught up in the hearsay and put extra stress on me because she never came back with any news, instead, Vet would only encourage and uplift me. The compassion that she showed me was from a place of hurt. Vet was going through something in her own relationship and I knew without her mentioning it to me that when she encouraged and uplifted me, she was also encouraging and uplifting herself.

Vet finally relieved me so I can go to the restroom. Right upon entering the lady's room, my supervisor Ms. Sherrol called my name to stop me. I turned around while holding my tears back "yes ma'am." "Come here," she insisted. "What's wrong with you? what's wrong with your face?" I said "I'm ok Ms. Sherrol" She then says "go ahead in there and do what you need to do, clean your face and come to my desk on the floor". I couldn't say anything but "yes ma'am" as I walked into the restroom. Once I entered a stall, it felt like everything that I was holding onto to keep me going, fell through the cracks. I haven't cried since the beginning of my pregnancy when the foolishness first started so when I finally let it out, I felt like I was having a breakdown. "Father strengthen me" I cried until my head started hurting. After five or six minutes, I came out of the stall and wiped my face with a wet paper towel. Then I walked over to the wall mirror as I continued to wipe my face and just looked at my reflection. I began to pray, speak and encourage myself. I also had to remind myself of who I was. I waited a few more minutes until my eyes cleared up and I walked out feeling better than when I walked in.

When I got to the line, Ms.Sherrol was looking at me with a serious face and I walked over to her as she asked. "Are you okay?" Ms.Sherrol asked. "Yes, I'm ok," I replied. Ms.Sherrol then began to say as she always put me in the mind of Jenifer Lewis " I know you are hurting and it doesn't make it any better that you just had this man's baby or the fact that this is what you walk into coming back to work". I never told her what was wrong with me but she knew by the time I came out of the restroom. Ms. Sherrol continued, "I told them that I did not want any company on this line, time and time again we always have to run that girl off from over here". She stopped for a minute and asked "how is the baby doing?" I answered her by saying " he is fine, thank you for asking" "I want to tell you something, and don't you ever forget it"

Ms. Sherrol was about to go in on me. "Don't you ever again give that much power to a man. I am married and I don't give my husband that type of power over me. The only one that gets that type of power and control over me is God. No one gets that much from you, don't you understand that God is a jealous God? He caused this disruption in your life because no man on this earth is supposed to get what belongs to Him". I just shook my head in agreement with her as she finished "hold your head up and take care of your babies because they need you ok?" I said "yes ma'am, thank you" and walked back to my station.

There was absolutely nothing that I can say because she was right. I let the whole situation get the best of me and I lost focus. I felt charged up for a while until other things started to trigger me. Honestly, one day I would be up and then the next day I would be down. I was on a complete emotional roller coaster and it was a challenge to keep my mind where it needed to be.

CHAPTER 12

The Shifting

The encouragement my supervisor gave me was uplifting and helped put me back on track for a little while. It seemed like the heat was turning up, and the walls of life were coming in on me. I was hurt, humiliated, and exhausted from everything as a whole. Being on my job with all the drama was embarrassing and humiliating. Somedays, I just didn't want to go to work to look none of them people in the face. I was exhausted because I was battling to keep my mind in the right frame of mind and take care of my children with everything else.

One day while I was at work, the plant managers called a meeting. They announced they were about to lay off because peak season was ending. I wasn't worried about being laid off because they only were letting go of temporary employees. However, I was bothered when they announced the rest of us would be working every other week. They told us that human resources would be filing our unemployment compensation for weeks we were not working. Moving forward, they had us working like that for about two months, and we had not been receiving any unemployment. We all came to find out that Human Resources was not filing for us because we had to do it ourselves.

Unfortunately, my bills were getting behind. I was trying to stretch what I was getting paid, and it simply wasn't enough. I still had to pay for childcare whenever I did work. My lights got disconnected once because I was trying to keep from getting evicted. I had no food stamps to help because they got cut off when I worked adequate hours. Therefore, I had to buy food cash out, and I could not get any until the second month because I needed to show proof from the first month. The food we had stored ran out, and there were days that I sacrificed not eating just so my children could eat.

The bills were one thing, but being unable to feed my children was the most challenging reality I have ever faced. I tried to get emergency food stamps, and they said they no longer provide them. Social services no longer offer anything to help parents who are in dire need of feeding their children. I asked my mom to bring us something to eat once, but I never mentioned what was happening.

Surprisingly, my grandmother showed up at my house one afternoon with a box of food and some bags. I didn't ask anything about it because I knew nobody but the Lord who sent my grandmother with food. It was more than enough and gave me time to figure out something else. The following day, I made a WIC appointment for us to have something extra coming in. It wasn't a lot, but I made it work with what my grandmother bought us.

Rick sometimes called, claiming he wanted to check on us, but I knew he wanted to know what I had going on. Nevertheless, I asked Rick to buy the baby some diapers, and he started saying things I knew came from other people. Rick told me he would get Qadir some diapers when I gave him a blood test. I knew that was someone in his ear because Rick was weak-minded and always took on what other people started. I paid close attention to how Rick moved and did things because he would call in a pleasant tone and whenever I asked him to help with something, he would always say something about a DNA test so that he wouldn't have to put out to help with anything.

Despite how Rick treated us, Robin would still invite us to her house for events. I didn't have a problem with Rick's family;

we got along very well. I was very close with two of his aunts because they constantly checked on us and helped whenever possible. His cousins would always have my back and defend me because they knew all the confusion was coming from that distant cousin, Meranda.

On the Fourth of July, Robin called me to bring the kids to her house because she was cooking out, so I decided to take her up on her offer. It felt good to get away from the walls that were closing in on me, but after a few hours, I saw Meranda pulling up to the cookout, which blew my whole mood. She brought her baby, which was just a month older than mine. I believed she came just to be nosey and watch how everyone responded and interacted with Qadir and me. I would tell anyone that woman was on an assignment from her daddy, Satan.

Meranda got out of the car and spoke to everyone, and I just looked at her. Meranda sat with us as if there was not one impure motive, and even though I wasn't fully aware of my spiritual gifts then, I most definitely was able to see straight through that. Everyone remained the same; no one acted any differently as she hoped, not even Rick. I noticed Meranda was making slick remarks, trying to be funny, but no one fed into it. As the night approached, she started doing a lot of whispering and having side conversations with Rick. When everyone was getting ready to leave, I heard Meranda yell to Rick, " you riding back with me, right?" Rick did not respond because he caught onto what she was doing.

I was past irritated with the foolishness. I know Meranda was plotting and was trying to pull Rick into it. He was too ignorant to see her orchestrating situations to stir up confusion. I sat quietly under the tree that was in the yard and watched everything. I watched the side conversations, them passing the cell phone back and forth and Rick being a fool running around following her up.

The next time I saw him walk off to talk on the phone, I walked right behind him and caught the tail end of the conversation. "I'm going to catch a ride with Meranda to meet you," he said. "Rick," I called his name as he turned around, startled by surprise. "Your son needs some more diapers," I purposely waited for him to come out with a stupid response. As soon as he said, "sure, after the blood test," I snatched his phone out of his hands, threw it as far as I could into the backyard woods, and walked off. Rick was extremely upset about that phone, and I didn't care about how he felt or anybody else. I told the boys to get our stuff and get in the truck. Rick stood on the porch and started yelling, "you better go find your baby daddy," I kept my mouth closed because I did not want to disrespect his mother's house.

After getting in the car, I paused for a moment to breathe and calm down before pulling off. Meranda's face had satisfaction all over it when she decided to get in her car to leave. Once we were in the car, I turned to look at the boys and Quesaan was paying attention to everything. Quesaan was nine years old and said "Ma let's go, don't ask him for help with nothing no more. I'll make some money to take care of; I don't care if I have to rake yards." Tears filled my eyes just to hear the hurt and maturity in my son's voice. I was taken aback by his desire to protect and provide for us because he understood the concept of a man when Rick couldn't even understand it. I knew things needed to change, but I felt like I was losing control of my life.

No matter how much I smiled and looked happy, deep inside me, I was broken. I continued to go to work and tried to maintain everything without the pay from unemployment. I cashed in change that I was saving for hard times and even pawned all my jewelry to keep extra money in my pocket. I was trying to pray my way through, but the more I prayed, the harder life was squeezing me. I was tired, and the outward battles were becoming inward battles.

The mornings were a struggle and the days seemed to be longer. Just to get out of bed and go into that place, not knowing what I would be facing. One day I went to work, and the day went by smoothly. No one came to me with any questions or comments about Rick. The more I pulled away from him and the people he associated with, the less I thought about him. However, as everyone stopped to clean their areas before we left for the day, I sat my cell phone inside one of the pans with my parts. When our time was up, I clocked out to leave. Once I got outside, I realized I had left my phone.

I turned around to go back into the building to get it, and upon leaving back out, I saw Rick walking up to his lady friend with the biggest smile on his face. He appeared happy and excited to see her after working all day since she was no longer allowed to come over to our line. I wasn't expecting to see anything, but when I did, it felt like someone had punched me in the stomach. He didn't see me, but for some reason, I believe it was supposed to happen just the way that it did. When I got inside my vehicle, the tears started flowing again. I kept thinking about the smile on his face and wondered what I had done wrong. What did I do to deserve the mistreatment and betrayal I was getting? When I got home, I sat in the truck for a minute and noticed an eviction notice on the door. I took the children out of the car, and once we got into the house, I told them to get washed up and put their bed clothes on. The baby was asleep in his car seat, so I left him as he was. I looked at the eviction notice, and I felt so heavy from all the weight I was carrying and felt like I was holding onto my life by a thread. I was so broken and tired. I cried, and all I knew to do was pray, but I was getting tired of praying too. The battle within was becoming too unbearable for me. As my two oldest boys came into the room to tell me, they were done. I dried my face and played it off because I never wanted my children to see me weak. I sent them out of the room to watch tv and told them I'd be out to fix something to eat. I looked at the paper once more and said, "Lord, I don't know what you expect me to do, but I'm tired," I walked out of the room.

That was the end of my work week, so I made plans to use the following week to attempt to find another job. I called the landlord the next day to let them know my situation. We agreed that I would pay them something every week until I got caught up. The agreement was okay then, but it was just as hard as before. I found myself in situations of deciding if I should pay the rent or pay the light bill. Not to mention the other expenses I had, such as car insurance, phone bill, child care, and buying food, toiletries, and gas to get around. Whatever loose change I had, I cashed it in to use.

My back was against the wall regarding my situation at home and the humiliation at work. The fight became so great after I did all I could; I was sinking in depression. On the days I didn't have to work, I tried to motivate myself to do something different but ended up back in my shell which was my room. Sometimes I didn't have five dollars to my name to put gas in the tank to go anywhere, which still resulted in me being in the room. There have been days that I struggled to get out of bed, especially since it's been summer break. I struggled to keep myself together mentally and no one knew what went on inside of that house but us.

Some days were worse than others. There were days that I was so depressed, sleep was the only thing that eased my mind. Being awake just made my mind run all over and as time passed it got worse. Sometimes I couldn't even get up to feed my children. Quesaan was now ten, and he was mature enough to understand his mother was in a dark place. Quesaan would get up and feed his brothers when I couldn't do it. He would fix sandwiches, and noodles, or warm up something quick to feed him and Quansae plus he already knew how to make formula to feed Qadir. Quesaan would feed the baby and burp him, if Qadir was sleepy or needed to be cleaned and changed, he would bring him back to me. Sometimes Quesaan would come and turn my light on, because my room stayed dark, and he was saying "ma can you get up please?" I kept my room dark because that was the atmosphere that I was adapting to. I allowed everything that I was going through to cause me to sink so low that I couldn't function, and unclean spirits were trying to take over my mind.

The thoughts of different hurts, disappointments, abandonment issues from relationships, and even my father wore heavy on me. I became furious and resentful towards my father because he was not here to guide and teach me. I was mad that he was not here to protect me. I tried to be strong and handle my business because that's what I saw my mother do as a single mother but deep down, I was broken. I started feeling like if life were going to be this way, I would rather not be here. I was tired and had no more fight in me, but somehow, my mind was returning to what I knew about God. I knew He existed, I knew He made himself known to me before, and as those events came back to me, I cried out and asked the Lord to help me.

As the days went by, the weight became even heavier. I just felt like I couldn't take it anymore. I wanted to shut everything up and shut everything down. The thoughts, the pain, the stress, and the voices in my head, I wanted it all to stop. So later that evening, while my kids were with their grandmother, I sat on the side of my bed and prayed as the tears soaked my face and shirt. "God, I can't do this anymore; I don't want to leave my children, but as far as me, I just don't want to be here no more." "Father, I don't want to go to hell because I know I didn't give myself this life, I just don't know what else to do, and I keep praying to You, but it's more hurt adding to me. Please forgive me!"

I stood up to walk towards the medicine cabinet to get the oxycodone pills that I was prescribed after my cesarean. From what I remembered, there was at least a half bottle of pills left. Once I opened the bottle, only one pill was left. I was so angry that there was not enough in the bottle to take, so I threw the bottle into the mirror. I was furious there were not enough pills so I started tearing my room apart. I screamed and dropped down to my knees and said to God "what happened to my pills?" "Why are you keeping me here?" My head was pounding from crying and screaming, and I stayed on my knees at the side of the bed until I fell asleep. When I fell asleep, my body was in my house, but my spirit was standing in front of two giant double doors. I didn't know exactly what had happened but I wasn't afraid. Moreover, the doors were so tall that they made me look the size of an ant. Around the edges of the doors was a bright white light beaming outward. Everything else was white, but I could tell it was a heavenly place. It was peaceful and quiet, and a calmness came over me. When I woke up, I remained in the same place, in awe of where I was.

I wanted to know what was behind those giant double doors, but the Lord gave me enough to search Him out. What I was allowed to see gave me a little hope, even though I didn't understand why. About a week later, Rick's aunt Lorraine called me and told me the Holy Spirit was dealing with her about me. She then asked if I wanted to come to church with her, and I told her yes; I would go. The following weekend we stayed with her for church and my life had never been the same. After the man of God gave the word, he started ministering to people.

The Apostle looked at me and said, "ma'am can I pray for you?" I shook my head, yes, and I proceeded to go to the front. The Apostle said, "I don't know you, and you don't know me, right?" "Right," was my response. He said, "I've never seen you before. Have you seen me before?" I shook my head no to him. He said, "okay," And told me everything in detail about what I was going through and how people close to me had knives in my back. He even went as far as to say that God needs me in the kingdom. He looked me in my eyes and said, "you have kingdom work to do, and that's why God was preserving you." I had a face full of tears because I was already full of hurt inside. I have never had someone to prophesy to me and tell me about where I was, what happened to me, and where I was going in the future. The more I went to church, the more strength I gained.

My healing process had begun, and I was no longer affected the way I used to be by the relationship I was formally in. I learned to look at life through my spiritual eyes and realized that the whole situation was beneath me. I no longer got upset and cried, but all I could do was laugh at how everything turned around. I brought the genetics test kit from CVS pharmacy for the at-home DNA testing. We took our swab samples and sent them off to the laboratory. It took about a week for the results to come back via email. I was trying to be nice and do it this way to prevent putting child support on Rick. Most women would have signed them papers a long time ago but I was trying to give him the benefit of the doubt that once he gets his results, he would handle his responsibility, but I told him that if I did it through social services, they were going to put papers on him and I was not going to take it off.

A week later, the test results came back, and just like I said, it read 99.99% probability of paternity. When Rick saw it, his only response was, "ok, so you weren't lying," but he told Meranda about it. Rick's cousin Meranda said to him that I had rigged the test. Here we go again with the foolishness, I thought, but this time I confronted her. When Meranda was walking past my workstation, I called her and asked her to come here for a minute. When she arrived, I said, "if you ever wondered why I stopped talking to you, it's because of the confusion you had going on. Miranda responded, "I wasn't the only one saying things about you." I cut her off in a firm tone, "I don't care about what everybody else had to say; you were the one at my house, my appointments, and the hospital when I had my baby." "I even heard you in the hospital saying my baby was not his." "Now that we've done a test, you are saying I rigged it up." She said, "yes, I think you did something to the test." I nodded as if I agreed with her saying, okay, I rigged it."

I told Rick one more time that if I went to DSS(department of social services), I would not take the papers off of him. All he had to say was ok. I had never seen such a weak man, but I was cool. God was giving me strength, and I could deal with the issues head-on. I started processing the paperwork, and about three weeks later, we went in to do the DNA test at social services. Another three weeks passed, and the results were back. He received a copy at his address as well as I received a copy at my address. I opened the envelope, and it said 99.99% probability of paternity. I laughed and said aloud, "now go tell Meranda that with your stupid self." Rick called my phone maybe two hours after he got home and opened the mail. When I answered the phone, he just started talking and said, " so it is 99.99%, you were telling the truth, and I just want to say I'm sorry about everything I took you through". I said, "I just don't get how you let somebody else tell you that your son is not yours, like you didn't know what you were doing. From what I see, Meranda shouldn't be giving anyone advice on relationships. She was married, running around with two other men, and was pregnant when I was. Maybe that was her motive, to have everyone's attention on me so that they wouldn't see or question her. "Yeah, you are right, Tay" Rick replied. I had nothing else to say, so I told him I'd talk to him later.

As for me, I continued to go to church with Rick's aunt and became a member there. The next time the Apostle had a word for me, he told me that God was turning things around for me and would increase my finances. He also told me the Lord said to remain humble and quiet because the more they talked about me, the crazier they would make themselves look. I received every word the Apostle gave me, and I acted accordingly.

Things were changing drastically, and it started with my home. I moved from where I was living and went back home to my mother's house until my finances got back in alignment. While I was there, I prayed for stability. I prayed for a stable place of my own that I can buy so that I wouldn't stress about paying rent. God answered that prayer expeditiously, and blew my mind the way it happened. I never looked around for a place, but someone I knew called me to tell me that she knew someone with a mobile home for sale and said I came across their mind. The mobile home was very affordable and liveable. Next, I got a promotion on my job with a pay increase. So not only did I not have to worry about rent anymore, but I also got a pay increase.

God was proving Himself to me and letting me know He had my back. God also had my back when He sent the message for me to remain quiet and let people talk because He knew that something else was going on that was about to spew over. As the weeks passed with me minding my business, feeling good, and moving forward, surprisingly, I found out that Rick's new girlfriend was pregnant. Except for the fact that she was pregnant way before she met him and was trying to plant it on him. I laughed when the news came to me; I thanked God for giving me the strength to walk away from the mess. The focus of the people was no longer on me but on them and who was that woman's baby father. I was satisfied with being by myself and made my mind up to get right with God. Just when I made my mind up the enemy tried to tempt me by sending Rick back to me. He called me one evening saying he wanted to see his child, and being that I was at my mother's house, I told him to come on by. When he got to the house, he didn't even ask about his child because he was so adamant about asking me to come outside with him. I got so aggravated with him asking me I told him to let me get my shoes first. Upon opening the door, the Holy Spirit said so loud and clear to me, "do not go outside." It stopped me right in my tracks and my feet was planted right where they were. Rick kept talking cause he couldn't hear what I was hearing, and I'm sure I had an unusual expression on my face. He kept saying, "hello are you coming outside so I can talk to you or not?" All the while, I was standing there unexpressive because I was listening to what the Holy Spirit was telling me. About 15 seconds past of me zoning out and when the Lord stopped talking I came back to myself and said to Rick, "no, I'm not going outside; I'm going to get my baby ready for bed." He gave up and said ok and didn't have anything to say about his son. Nevertheless, I wasn't worried about him or anyone else for the matter. God kept his word concerning me and mine, and to this day, everybody else that took part in trying to destroy me, put their mouth on me, or even counted me out is witnessing how the Lord is working in my life.

Every time I go through a rough season of my life, I think of everything my God has brought me through, and I am reminded that I am never alone. I have grown in ways I never thought I would've grown, and there is so much more to me that still is yet to come.

As it is written in 1 Corinthians 2:9 *Eye hath not seen, nor ear heard, neither have entered into the heart of man, the things which God hath prepared for them that love him.*

My heart will be forever grateful for all that the Most High God has done for me. He had rescued me when there was no other way, and had shown me love when I did not have it within myself, I will forever dedicate my life to Him.

<u>Overview</u>

When I look back over my life, I wish I had a rewind button to start over again. I am sure most of you feel the same way. I always knew that I was different, and I knew that I wanted life to be different for me. I wasn't conscious of what I was doing, but I was looking for my life to be different through a man. I looked at how my family mainly consisted of women and their children, and no fathers or husbands were around to do their part.

I understood that much as a young girl, but my difference wasn't that type of different. My difference was not in a man but in God. He would've made a difference in my life only if I had searched for Him and kept pressing after He tried to get my attention and awaken me. I thought that if I showed this guy or guy, I was a keeper, he would change, but that wasn't my reality. I did not get that capacity of wisdom until after I went through the hurt and pain. I realized that I was someone special to Christ and that He would release who He thought would be fit and who He trusted to take care of His chosen daughter.

Furthermore, I had to learn to forgive myself and move forward. We all wish we would've done something differently, and we always say if I would've known then what I know now, but everything has a purpose. I didn't know my own story, but God knows. The devil even got a glimpse and tried to destroy me before I came into the knowledge of Christ, but it was for my good. *Gen.50:20 NKJ says, "But as for you, you meant evil against me; but God meant it good.*

God allows us to go through different experiences to appreciate Him and what He has done for us and be relatable to help others. God will even use us to help those that have harmed us. There were nights when God woke me out of my sleep to pray for or minister to some of the very same people I spoke of in this book. He would give me insight into something and wake me to stand in the gap for them. Did I want to? No. Was praying for someone who hurt me easy? No. I even told God it wasn't fair, and asked why should I pray for them, but I had to reach a place of maturity and realize that it wasn't about me. It's about God and what He is trying to do in the next person's life, and I wouldn't wish hell on my worst enemy.

Sometimes God would even allow people to hurt us and then change our lives so that those people can see God's glory in our lives and it will cause them to have a repentant changed heart. Some people hurt us because they see already see it and they will not be able to move forward or achieve things in Him until they come back and get it right. Nevertheless, we are vessels used for His glory, whichever way He allows it to go and we have to realize that. I do wish things would have gone differently for me but do I have regrets? No for three reasons. The first is because He kept me. God knows my ending and He knows what He has invested in me. Secondly, I got everything I needed from those abusive relationships. Whether it was physical abuse, manipulation, or gaslighting. I learned something from them all. Finally, I am relatable, and I can reach back and pull others out of that place of darkness.

The Lord is intentional about everything concerning us. He wants everyone to know Him or get to know Him in a new way but He will not force Himself on anyone. He will allow things to happen to get our attention and open our eyes but it's up to us to seek Him. He has given us all free will but when you make your mind up to accept Him into your heart, everything will begin to unfold. I must add, there is no such thing as waiting until everything is in place, or waiting until you fix certain things about yourself. We are imperfect people that need a perfect God and if we can do everything perfectly already, there would be no need for God.

<u>Prayer</u>

Heavenly Father, I come before you with all thanksgiving and praise. As humble as I know how, I thank you for my life. Thanking you for keeping, shielding, and protecting me when you didn't have to. Lord, I am not perfect and I don't pretend to be. I ask that you help me to be the person that you created me to be in this earthly realm. I ask that you remove the scales from my eyes so that I can see life through your eyes. Give me the capacity to obtain divine wisdom, knowledge, and understanding. Lord give me your heart in exchange for mines and make me more sensitive to your spirit. Give me the spirit of discernment. I want to be more like you so help me think more like you, help me to speak more like you. Guide my footsteps the rest of the days of my life and increase my faith in you. In Jesus name, Amen!

Made in the USA
Columbia, SC
10 March 2023